Atlantic Canada Today

THE ATLANTIC PROVINCES ECONOMIC COUNCIL

The Council was formed in 1954. It is an independent, not-for-profit, private corporation with a membership including large and small businesses, labour organizations, government and community agencies, industry organizations, members of the academic community, and individuals. APEC's primary objective is to promote the economic development of the four Atlantic provinces. This goal is pursued through development of public policy, analysis and comment on emerging issues, delivering a unique information service to members, and promoting economic cooperation among the Atlantic provinces and the federal government.

APEC maintains a regular publications program, which charts the course of the regional economy in detail by sector and province, and analyses topics of current and potential concern to Atlantic Canada. More information on publications, and on membership in the Council, can be obtained from APEC, 5121 Sackville Street, Suite 500, Halifax, Nova Scotia, Canada B3J 1K1, (902) 422-6516.

Atlantic Canada Today

Atlantic Provinces Economic Council

Formac Publishing Limited
Halifax 1987

Canadian Cataloguing in Publication Data

Main entry under title:
Atlantic Canada Today

ISBN 0-88780-059-9

1. Atlantic Provinces - Economic conditions - 1945 — .
I. Atlantic Provinces Economic Council

HC117.A75A7 1987 330.9715'04 C87-094784-2

Credits   6231/

The quotations on pages and in chapter one are reproduced with permission
of the Oxford University Press.
Figure 3.1, Table 4.1, the quotation on page 60 in chapter four, and the
quotation on page 113 of chapter ten, are all reproduced with permission of
the Minister of Supply and Services Canada.

Formac Publishing Company Limited
5359 Inglis Street
Halifax, Nova Scotia
B3H 1J4

Printed and bound in Canada

TABLE OF CONTENTS

Chapter		Page

ERRATA

Table 4.2, page 48, "Salted and/or Dried Fish" should be 88.1% of the Canadian total, not 8.1% as shown.

Figure 4.3, pages 55-56, the shading in the legend has been transposed. White is vessels of more than 25 tonnes, the grey screen is vessels of 25 tonnes or less.

Table 8.2, page 100, employment in fish products manufacturing in New Brunswick should read 3,829 and 13.4% of all manufacturing, not 5,235 and 18.3% as shown.

Figure 10.4, page 125, the legend should read, from top to bottom, Atlantic Provinces (solid black), British Columbia (including Territories) (lighter screen), Ontario (darker screen), Prairie Provinces (cross hatch), and Quebec (white).

Table 11.2, page 132, the last column should read, from top to bottom, 937, 211, 89, 7,676, 398, 77, 1,135, and 7,475. The next to last row should read, from left to right, 747, 892, 117, 118, 1,471, 1,902, 1,011, and 1,135.

Table 11.3, page 132, the row of numbers shown "As % of all employed" for Newfoundland and Labrador is in fact "Payroll ($ million)". Numbers in the row to the right of "As % of all employed" should then read, from left to right, 4.7, 13.2, 1.4, and 19.3.

LIST OF TABLES

viii

LIST OF FIGURES

ACKNOWLEDGEMENTS

APEC is pleased to acknowledge the financial contributions provided for this project by several corporate sponsors. They are:
  Air Canada
  Bank of Montreal
  Esso Resources Canada Limited
  Marine Atlantic
  Maritime Telegraph and Telephone
  McCain Foods Limited
  Petro-Canada

PRESIDENT'S FOREWORD

The Atlantic Provinces Economic Council engages in many activities in the pursuit of promoting the economic development of the region. A large part of these efforts is devoted to providing timely information. This book illustrates a major example of that effort.

Atlantic Canadians respresent less than 10% of the national population. Distances within the region, however, are greatly extended by the incidence of salt water, so much so that the region encompasses a total area greater than that of Ontario. These distances exert a major influence on the regional economy, and are one of the reasons why this economy is more diverse than generally realised.

Requests for information on economic matters are constantly directed to APEC from both inside and outside the region. An objective of this book is to provide a useful reference handbook to answer some of these inquiries.

While many people have contributed to this work, most credit must go to Maurice Mandale, APEC Senior Economist, who has nurtured it from basic research, through many revisions, to final publication.

Special thanks must go to the Nova Scotia office of the Atlantic Canada Opportunity Agency, and the Nova Scotia Department of Development, which jointly funded final publication under the Canada-Nova Scotia Economic Development Planning Subsidiary Agreement.

Robert A. Stuart
August 1987

EDITOR'S PREFACE

This is the third book prepared by staff of the Atlantic Provinces Economic Council to include the words Atlantic Canada Today in its title. The earlier editions came out in 1969 and 1977. This volume bears passing resemblance to its illustrious predecessors in that it addresses the broad structure of the Atlantic economy and some of the issues which surround it. It is not, however, a revision of previous editions, but is a completely new book, originally researched and written from scratch.

To make it easier to use as a handbook, we have adopted a sector by sector approach. If this appears rather pedestrian, it allows individual chapters to stand alone, more or less. This should not obscure the many linkages which characterise the regional economy, particularly between resource extraction and subsequent processing of these resources. We have also attempted to inject elements of a textbook to explain some of the basic points of economics by local example.

One of the fundamental aims of economics writing is to take information (which many regard as inherently uninteresting, some would say dull) and make it understandable to a wider readership. This may be achieved partly by anecdote, partly by graphic illustration, and partly by knowing when to stop and refer people, if interested, to other publications. Most chapters have a brief section of further reading to assist this last endeavour.

We have attempted to be comprehensive, but not exhaustive. Many readers would probably like to see better treatment of public finances, others more emphasis on small business in Atlantic Canada; other topics could be found, and may even be addressed in future editions. The extent to which we have succeeded in our aims must be determined by those who read the book, and who take pains to let us know what they think.

Many people have been involved in preparation of the book over the rather long time it took. They include Elizabeth Beale (formerly of APEC, now a consulting economist); J. Fred Morley; Bill Steele (formerly of APEC, now with the federal government); and Glenna Jenkins. APEC President, Bob Stuart bullied and cajoled us along, and in the end showed exemplary patience. Andrew Meade helped in data assembly and several updates in the final stages. Several generations of typists and word processors did several drafts, mostly with forbearance and efficiency. Lois Duffy, APEC's office manager, performed many tasks of coordination during the final stages especially. We accept the inevitability that there are inaccuracies in the book, and would appreciate a brief (and we hope courteous) word from people who identify them.

Maurice Mandale
Senior Economist,
August 1987

CHAPTER 1

Atlantic Canada: An Introduction

There are four provinces in Atlantic Canada:

- Newfoundland and Labrador
- Prince Edward Island
- Nova Scotia
- New Brunswick

The last three are frequently referred to collectively as the Maritime provinces. Nova Scotia and New Brunswick were founding members of the Canadian Confederation in 1867; Prince Edward Island joined Canada in 1873. Newfoundland (usually referred to thus rather than by its full name) retained its status as a British colony until 1949, when it became Canada's tenth province.

Location

The provinces are in northeastern North America, pointing towards Europe. The region, extending over 17 degrees both of latitude and longitude, contains 539,101 square kilometres of land and fresh water (Table 1.1). Labrador accounts for 54% of this total. Salt water covers a large part of the region, washing some 16,000 km of shoreline.

While references to "the region" will recur throughout this book, this does not imply that Atlantic Canada is a homogeneous area. As R.C. Harris and J. Warkentin comment:

TABLE 1.1: APPROXIMATE LAND AND FRESH WATER AREAS, ATLANTIC PROVINCES AND CANADA

	Land	Fresh Water	Total	Percent of Total
	— square kilometers			— % —
Newfoundland and Labrador	370,485	34,032	404,517	4.1
Island	106,614	5,685	112,299	1.1
Labrador	263,871	28,347	292,218	3.0
Prince Edward Island	5,657	—	5,657	0.1
Nova Scotia	52,841	2,650	55,491	0.6
New Brunswick	72,092	1,344	73,436	0.7
Atlantic Canada	501,075	38,026	539,101	5.4
Canada	9,167,165	755,165	9,922,330	100.0

Source: *Canada Year Book 1980–81.*

> This is a very complex region. It has no unifying configuration of physical features, and even the surrounding sea provides a matrix rather than a focus. There is no centralization of economic activity or function, no rich heartland. If there is any unity, it is a unity of mutual problems arising from the attempt to wrest from modest resources a standard of living roughly equivalent to that of the rest of Canada and the United States.[1]

Atlantic Canada is physically diverse. The well-manicured aspect of much of Prince Edward Island and the farming areas of Nova Scotia and New Brunswick contrast sharply with the ruggedness of Newfoundland and Labrador. Climate ranges widely, too, from Arctic (boreal) in northern Labrador to temperate throughout much of the Maritime region. Although weather derives mainly from continental systems moving eastwards, these are modified by the ocean; winter weather is usually milder than further west, summer weather is usually cooler.

Ocean currents also have their influence on weather. The Gulf Stream passes a little off Nova Scotia, *skirting* the region rather than *washing* it in the way it does much of northwest Europe. This warm ocean current, therefore, exercises less influence on the region's weather than in Europe. This helps explain why Halifax, although at the same latitude as the south of France, does not have the same weather.

The Gulf Stream does help ensure that the southern shores of Nova Scotia are ice-free all year, unlike the Gulf of St Lawrence to the north. The cold Labrador current carries ice down to the southern parts of Newfoundland each year, and where it meets the warmer Gulf Stream waters around the Grand Banks, fog banks frequently form.

Large areas of ocean should not be regarded as so much wasted space. Their fish enticed the first important interest by Europeans, and submarine hydrocarbon resources offer bright prospects in the late twentieth century. But the ocean also exacts its price. It makes transportation difficult, particularly during the winter months, because of a highly irregular configuration of land and water; and it does not give up its resources easily, as both fishermen and oil exploration workers can attest.

Atlantic Canada is well located for transporting goods by water. It is near European and eastern North American markets along the Great Circle shipping route of the north Atlantic; and it has access to the heart of North America along the St Lawrence-Great Lakes shipping lanes.

It follows that the region's ports are vital parts of the economic infrastructure. Indeed, the three biggest urban centres (Halifax-Dartmouth, Saint John, and St John's) are all port cities. They were settled first for strategic and commercial reasons around good natural harbours. The fact that this meant building substantially on rock, often in a confined space, has posed interesting challenges as population grew and demand for housing and social capital expanded.

Principal Physical Features

There are three principal physiographic features represented in Atlantic Canada:

- The Canadian Shield (Labrador)
- The Appalachian Mountains (the Maritime provinces and the island of Newfoundland)
- The Continental Shelf

The Canadian Shield. Much of Labrador is considered part of the Shield, a platform of extremely old rocks with rather monotonous relief. Labrador ranges around 300 metres above sea level generally, although local elevation and relief is much higher than this. In the Torngat Mountains in northern Labrador, Atlantic Canada's highest point occurs at 1,652 metres. Elsewhere, deeply incised rivers offer potential to generate electricity where they tumble over barriers along their course, as at Churchill Falls. The shield is also economically significant for its mineral deposits and forests. Much of the land remains undeveloped, however, because of remoteness and climate.

The Appalachian Mountains. These extend the length of eastern North America from Georgia to Newfoundland. They are not a single, simple range, but a series of complex and roughly parallel ridges. The great age of the mountains means that millions of years of erosion by ice, water, and other agents have worn down the high peaks; only the stumps remain. One of these "stumps" is Mount Carleton in northern New Brunswick, which is 820 metres high, and in an area of valuable mineralisation. Peaks reach 814 metres in western Newfoundland, and 532 metres in Nova Scotia's Cape Breton Highlands, two areas where mountains rise steeply and spectacularly from the sea.

In the Maritimes, the upland ranges are interspersed with lower sedimentary basins, the biggest of which rings the southern part of the Gulf of St Lawrence including all of Prince Edward Island. No part of this province rises above 142 metres. These lowlands contain some of the region's best farmland. Extensive coal deposits are also associated with these basins in Nova Scotia and New Brunswick.

The Continental Shelf. There are two main parts to this submarine shelf: the Gulf of St Lawrence and the Atlantic Banks. Both are extensions of the land under the sea, and were, in fact, land in the not-too-distant past, albeit covered by very thick ice. The shelf extends outwards to a depth of about 100 fathoms (200 metres), not encountered off parts of Newfoundland until almost 300 nautical miles offshore. The relative shallowness of the shelf throughout the region provides superb habitat for large numbers of commercially important fish species, especially on a series of banks off Newfoundland and Nova Scotia. These shallow waters also make undersea oil and gas exploration easier.

An extension of the northwest Atlantic between New Brunswick and Nova Scotia has formed the Bay of Fundy, a long arm of the sea that gets narrower towards its head. The resultant compression of the water, which sweeps in twice daily with the tides, produces the highest tidal ranges in the world, varying up to 16 metres under the right combination of lunar phenomena.

A Brief Economic History

The [Atlantic] region has never controlled its own economic destiny, and since the mid-nineteenth century it has been affected even more strongly by its hapless relationship with other parts of North America. In the eighteenth century it was a precarious border territory in the struggles between the French and the English in North America; in the early nineteenth century it achieved a strong trading role in the Atlantic based on its regional resources and strategic location. Yet as the century advanced the region was affected ever more strongly by the continent, even though it was outside the main thrust of North American industrial development.[2]

Early Contacts. Atlantic Canada's location has moulded much of its history. As the part of North America closest to Europe, it is a logical first landfall on north Atlantic crossings. The first visitors were Viking adventurers, sailing out of Iceland or Greenland. They wintered at l'Anse aux Meadows at Newfoundland's northern tip about the year 1000, and this may be the land described in the Vinland Saga. The sagas also mentioned plentiful shoals of fish in the seas.

Once this new land had been found, Europeans promptly forgot about it for several centuries. Population in the Old World was still relatively small in relation to its resources. Even when westward exploration resumed towards the end of the fifteenth century, it was to discover an easier passage to the Far East and its valuable spice trade. John Cabot landed in Cape Breton in 1497 (the exact location is unknown) and apparently christened the land Cathay. The Cabots' voyages confirmed the sagas' accounts of seas teeming with fish, but Europeans concentrated their interest in the New World on precious metals, particularly in Latin America.

Cartier's voyages to eastern Canada (he concentrated mainly on the St Lawrence River) were also in search of gold. These explorations set the stage for a powerful French influence in interior North America. In the subsequent struggle between English and French for control of the continent, Atlantic Canada played a strategic part.

The Cod Fishery. European interest in the Atlantic region was eventually aroused by the fish on the Atlantic Banks. We do not know exactly when fishermen were first drawn past Icelandic fishing grounds; their trips possibly predated those of the well-known explorers. We know that population growth in fifteenth century Europe began to exert upward pressure on the price of food. Higher prices for fish induced fishing boats to search further afield in the quest for profits and stimulated an expansion of the fishing fleet; it was relatively cheap and easy to enter a small-boat fishery.

About 1550, dry-curing of the fish began to replace on-boat wet-curing, the method favoured by pioneering French fishermen. Dry-curing was both more efficient and gave a higher-quality product. However, the fish had to be taken ashore, where they were put on wooden staging. The drying was speeded by fires, and the first penetration of Newfoundland's forests provided wood for this purpose. The first semi-permanent settlements began.

This first cod fishery has been characterised as a staples economy, a theme that underlies Atlantic development. Dependence on staple products (essentially raw materials) means dependence on commerce. Distant markets become the engines of local economic growth and prosperity.

The early fishery was run from home ports, and did not encourage more than transient settlement. Even by the mid-1700s only 6,000 people lived in small land-locked communities around the coast of Newfoundland, after some two centuries of enterprise. As early as 1603, however, a French settlement on marshes around the Bay of Fundy combined farming with fishing and wood-cutting. About 10,000 people lived here just prior to expulsion by the British in 1755.

A Century of Conflict. Strategic concerns predominated in the region during the eighteenth century, as French and British exported their hostilities from Europe to begin their struggle for North America. This, in turn, was a much greater spur to settlement than the fishery. The French established their fortress at Louisbourg in 1714, hoping to attract new settlement in its hinterland in Isle Royale (now Cape Breton Island). The choice of location for the fortress was unfortunate; remote from established French settlement around the Bay of Fundy, in the middle of marshes on an open and rather inhospitable stretch of shoreline. The British established a military centre on the fine natural harbour at Halifax in 1749, and encouraged sympathetic civilian settlement of northern Europeans and New Englanders nearby, both to counter the established Acadian settlement on the Bay of Fundy and to promote local supplies of agricultural produce and other essentials required by the military base.

The British consolidated their position by the brutal dispersal of the Acadians in 1755. This successful early settlement had been based on marshland agriculture protected from the Fundy tides by a sophisticated system of dikes. The Acadians had largely been ignored by France, and they had developed into a reasonably autonomous and prosperous society. Large numbers were forcibly deported by the British to present-day Louisiana; their descendants in the southern United States today, the Cajuns, still retain some French in everyday speech. Others took to the woods, and gradually regrouped over subsequent years in areas considered on the margins of British influence (principally in eastern and northern New Brunswick). In 1758 the British seized French lands in Ile St-Jean (settled since 1719), which was renamed Prince Edward Island in 1799.

6

The Treaty of Paris in 1763 gave Britain all of Canada except the islands of St Pierre and Miquelon south of Newfoundland. Almost immediately, Britain faced rebellion in its American colonies. A fundamental split developed between the colonists on both sides of the border. Those who supported the rebellion prevailed in the American colonies (to the gratification of their French allies, recently displaced by the British); those who wished to remain under Britain formed the majority of settlers in the present-day Maritime provinces, and were augmented by a stream of defeated Loyalists from the south. In fact, the degree of dissent in the Canadian colonies against an arrogant and uncaring home government across the ocean was such that only narrowly did they avoid becoming the fourteenth star on the flag of the new republic. Had this happened, British influence in North America would have been confined to Newfoundland.[3]

A Century of Settlement and Prosperity. New land-hungry migrants from Europe began streaming across the Atlantic towards the end of the eighteenth century, and the flow swelled during the nineteenth. Atlantic Canada was at least a first foothold for many of these immigrants. The regional population at century's start was about 100,000, but had swelled to 900,000 by 1900. The century also ushered in a period of general prosperity based on a burst of mercantilism. Diversion of foreign ships from American ports after the Embargo Act of 1807 (an act of retaliation by the Americans against various provocations of both Britain and France) saw Atlantic merchants recover a great deal of trade with Britain's West Indian colonies, formerly lost to American shipping.

About the same time, Napoleon turned to blockade in Europe as an alternative means to defeat the British in their war. This threatened supplies of Baltic timber, essential for the British navy. The North Atlantic timber trade began, based on the untouched forests of eastern Canada. This new industry provided a valuable link between primary fishing and trapping, and an economy based on agriculture and manufacture. Aspiring farmers had their first cash crop in the form of trees, and an opportunity to assemble enough capital to begin cultivation of the newly cleared land. Ships were needed to carry the timber to market. The era of wind, wood and water began. Both the Royal Bank of Canada and the Bank of Nova Scotia were founded at this time in Halifax, a reflection of the accumulation of capital in the region both from timber and trade.

Settlement proceeded during the century, and not only in the Atlantic region. Increased settlement throughout North America provided opportunities for the region to supply the process of internal expansion, but, unfortunately, the process itself moved the continental centre of gravity further and further away from its northeastern extremity. Fishing remained the backbone of Newfoundland, made a Crown colony in 1824. The three Maritime provinces developed a mixture of fishing, forestry, shipbuilding, and general manufacture.

A brief flirtation with free trade with the United States (called reciprocity then) ended abruptly in 1866. This had enhanced general prosperity, and its loss had the effect of persuading Upper and Lower Canada to join Nova Scotia and New Brunswick in Confederation in 1867. This was a watershed in Canadian history. Sir John A. Macdonald's National Policy of 1879 was intended to put some order into economic expansion. Western resources were to be developed, and the national manufacturing base was to expand behind a national tariff. Maritime industries were to share in this expansion by favourable freight rates for their goods shipped to central markets on the new Intercolonial railway.

As iron and steel hulls began to replace wood in shipbuilding after about mid-century (see Figure 1.1) so resources moved between industries in Atlantic Canada. Steel mills and railcar manufacture developed as railways were built to serve the emerging Prairie wheat economy. The tariff afforded protection to allow sugar refining, glassmaking and textiles to develop. There was a smooth transition to a relatively diverse economic base from the old wood, wind, and water economy.

Meanwhile, central manufacturing developed apace behind the tariff wall to such an extent that overcapacity resulted. Surpluses were dumped on Maritime markets, and local producers were either absorbed by outside concerns, or simply went out of business. Regional banks were also absorbed by outside interests and moved, or took the initiative themselves and transferred their capital to the emerging manufacturing powerhouse of southern Ontario.

In the early years of the twentieth century, the federal government began to raise the freight rates paid by Maritime shippers. This part of the Confederation agreement had originally been to compensate for diversion of Maritime trade from its natural north-south direction to an east-west direction once the tariff was in place. By the time Maritime industries had organised to fight the rate increases (the Maritime Rights Movement of the 1920s) the First World War had come and gone, post-war recession was well established, and the effects of higher freight rates were seen in permanently lost manufacturing jobs in the region (Table 1.2).

The Twentieth Century. Until well after the Second World War, any new developments in secondary industry in Atlantic Canada were essentially involved with processing the region's resources, as in pulp and paper manufacture. Personal incomes began to diverge from the national

FIGURE 1.1: NUMBERS OF NEW SHIPS REGISTERED IN PRINCE EDWARD ISLAND BY DECADE, 1820–1920

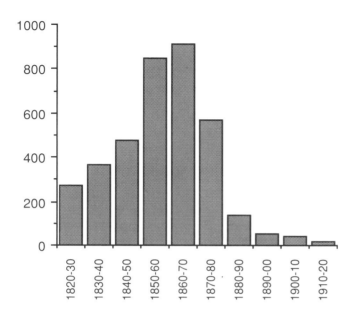

Source: L.C. Callbeck, "Economic and Social Development since Confederation", in *Canada's Smallest Province: A History of P.E.I.* Edited by F.W.P. Bolger, 1973

TABLE 1.2: MANUFACTURING EMPLOYMENT IN SELECTED TOWNS IN NOVA SCOTIA AND NEW BRUNSWICK, 1920 and 1926

	1920	1926
Amherst	2,267	735
Dartmouth	1,581	946
Halifax	7,171	3,287
New Glasgow	2,610	611
Sydney	2,929	2,053
Truro	1,080	778
Moncton	3,061	2,133
Saint John	4,630	3,394

Source: *Canada Year Book, 1922–23* and *1929*.

An Introduction

average, and chronic economic disparities became normal. There was a burst of energy during the Second World War, when the ports once again became bustling centres of activity, but this was followed by precipitous economic decline leading to mass emigration. This began from rural to urban areas within the region, and then turned increasingly to emigration to other parts of Canada and the United States. This tended to take the best and most innovative individuals from the region, as they were forced to move to find work.

The post-war period has been distinguished by a growing awareness of the economic inequities which exist in Canada, which were not in the spirit of a confederation of equal partners. A succession of policies, some successful, many more less so, have reflected governments' concern over these inequities. The region now has a more diverse economic base, which still incorporates substantial reliance on the processing of natural resources. The single major new development has been the emergence of a dominant service sector, more or less in line with the evolution of the wider North American economy. Many of the characteristics of the Atlantic economy in the late twentieth century will be explored in subsequent chapters of this book.

Footnotes

1. R.C. Harris and J. Warkentin, *Canada before Confederation: A Study in Historical Geography.* (1974, Oxford University Press.) p. 169.

2. Harris and Warkentin, *op. cit.* p. 170.

3. This largely untold story of the North American rebellion features in several of the novels of Thomas H. Raddall (notably *His Majesty's Yankees*) and his book *Halifax: Warden of the North*, published by McClelland and Stewart, 1971.

Further Reading

Easterbrook, W.T. and H.G.J. Aitken, *Canadian Economic History.* Toronto: Macmillan Company of Canada, 1956. Reprinted 1978.

Easterbrook, W.T. and M.H. Watkins (eds.) *Approaches to Canadian Economic History: A Selection of Essays*. Carleton Library No. 31. Toronto: the Macmillan Company of Canada, 1967. Note especially the papers by W.A. Mackintosh, "Economic Factors in Canadian History"; H.A. Innis, "The Importance of Staple Products" and "The Fur Trade"; A.R.M. Lower, "The Trade in Square Timber"; M.H. Watkins, "A Staple Theory of Economic Growth"; B. Hammond, "Banking in Canada before Confederation"; and K. Buckley, "Capital Formation in Canada, 1896-1930".

Harris, R.C. and J. Warkentin, *Canada before Confederation: A Study in Historical Geography*. Historical Geography of North America Series. New York, London, and Toronto: Oxford University Press, 1974. Note especially chapters 1, 2 and 5.

Innis, H.A., *The Cod Fishery: The History of an International Economy*, Revised edition, Canadian University Paperbacks No. 212. Toronto: University of Toronto Press, 1954.

Morison, S.E., *The European Discovery of America: The Northern Voyages A.D. 500 - 1600*. New York: Oxford University Press, 1971.

CHAPTER 2

Atlantic Canada: Some Basic Numbers

Population, Density and Distribution. About 2.3 million people live in Atlantic Canada in the late 1980s, or 9% of the Canadian total (Table 2.1). The national population has grown at a consistently faster rate than the regional population since 1851, both as the Canadian territory expanded and as economic fortunes in other parts of the country outpaced those in the Atlantic region. Although there were almost four times as many people living in Atlantic Canada in 1986 than in 1851, the Canadian population increased by about ten times over the same period (Figure 2.1).

The average density of population in Atlantic Canada in 1986 was 4.2 persons per square kilometre compared with a national average of 2.6 persons per square kilometre. This density rises to 9.6 persons in New Brunswick, 15.6 persons in Nova Scotia, and 22.2 persons in Prince Edward Island. Consideration of Labrador pulls down Newfoundland's average to 1.4 people per square kilometre.

Communication and settlement took on a linear aspect early, either along the coast or along river valleys. Water provided the easiest form of travel, and the sea was the source of principal economic activity. Many outports in Newfoundland are still isolated overland; travel to and from other communities is still by sea. Only where agriculture developed in the Maritimes did relatively dense networks of roads follow.

TABLE 2.1: POPULATION, ATLANTIC PROVINCES AND CANADA, 1851–1986

	Newfoundland and Labrador (1)	Prince Edward Island	Nova Scotia	New Brunswick	Canada
			– thousands –		
1851		62.7(2)	276.9	193.8	2,436.3
1861		80.9	330.9	252.0	3,229.6(3)
1871		94.0	387.8	285.6	3,689.3
1881		108.9	440.6	321.2	4,324.8
1891		109.1	450.4	321.3	4,833.2(4)
1901		103.3	459.6	331.1	5,371.3
1911		93.7	492.3	351.9	7,206.6
1921		88.6	523.8	387.9	8,787.9
1931		88.0	512.8	408.2	10,376.8
1941		95.0	578.0	457.4	11,506.7
1951	361.4	98.4	642.6	515.7	14,009.4
1961	457.9	104.6	737.0	597.9	18,238.2
1971	522.1	111.6	789.0	634.6	21,568.3
1981	567.7	122.5	847.4	696.4	24,343.2
1986	568.3	126.6	873.2	710.4	25,354.1

Notes: 1) Census for Newfoundland before 1951 were not always held regularly. Population for Newfoundland in various years was 75,000 (1836); 124,000 (1857); 147,000 (1869); 161,000 (1874); 197,000 (1884); 202,000 (1891); 221,000 (1901); 243,000 (1911); 263,000 (1921); 290,000 (1936); 322,000 (1945); and 354,000 (1949).
2) For 1848.
3) Includes Manitoba for the first time.
4) Includes Saskatchewan and Alberta for the first time.

Sources: Censuses of Canada; *Historical Statistics of Newfoundland and Labrador* (1970).

FIGURE 2.1: CUMULATIVE PERCENTAGE RATE OF POPULATION GROWTH, ATLANTIC PROVINCES AND CANADA, 1851–1986

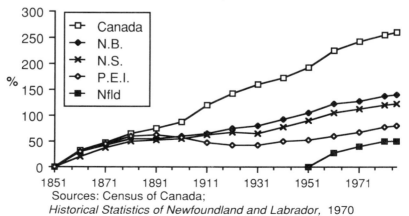

Sources: Census of Canada;
Historical Statistics of Newfoundland and Labrador, 1970

Atlantic Canada Today

FIGURE 2.2: RURAL-URBAN DISTRIBUTION OF POPULATION, ATLANTIC PROVINCES AND CANADA

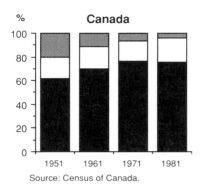

Canada

- Rural Farm
- Rural Non-Farm
- Urban

Source: Census of Canada.

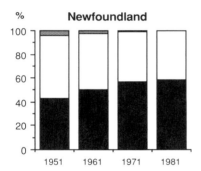

Newfoundland

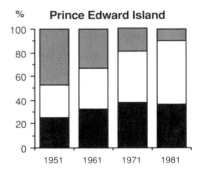

Prince Edward Island

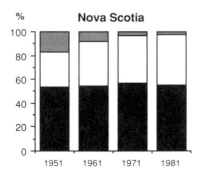

Nova Scotia

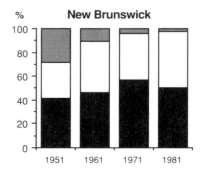

New Brunswick

Rural and Urban Population. Atlantic population, even in the 1980s, demonstrates a close attachment to resources by being markedly less urban than Canada as a whole. The extreme is reached in Prince Edward Island, almost two-thirds rural compared to about one-quarter nationally (Figure 2.2). The other three provinces are also substantially more rural as defined by census counts.

Many people classified as rural dwellers in the census, however, inhabit those parts of rural municipalities adjacent to, or within easy commuting distance of, incorporated urban areas. This, in part, explains the generally increasing proportion of the Atlantic population classified as "rural non-farm" between 1951 and 1981. In the first place, the decline of farming as a source of employment (only Prince Edward Island retained an appreciable farm population in 1981) caused rural people to seek non-farm jobs. In the second place, rising incomes and increased personal mobility have allowed many people to combine an urban income with rural dwelling. This may be easier in Atlantic Canada than elsewhere, as towns and cities are smaller and give way more rapidly to countryside.

This enhanced degree of urban orientation does not obscure the fact, however, that Atlantic Canada is probably nearer its rural roots than most other parts of Canada. The biggest urban concentration in the region is Halifax-Dartmouth, with a modest 295,000 inhabitants. Charlottetown, although a provincial capital, has less than 50,000 inhabitants. Newfoundland's biggest urban-centred region is St John's, with about 162,000 people. New Brunswick has three significant urban-centred regions - Saint John, Moncton and Fredericton - but only the first of these exceeds 100,000 people.

Ethnic Background. The vast majority of people in Atlantic Canada can trace their ancestry to either the British Isles or France (Figure 2.3). Three of the provinces are predominantly British or Irish in origin, while New Brunswick is more than one-third French. There are also pockets of French-speaking people in Prince Edward Island and Nova Scotia. There is a small but significant black population in Nova Scotia (about 30,000), including descendants of slaves who came north with Loyalist settlers in the late eighteenth century. Between 14,000 and 15,000 native people also live in the region.

Atlantic Canada has not become as cosmopolitan as Canada as a whole, where more than one-quarter of all people in 1981 had neither British nor French roots. Most of the recent immigration that has contributed to this trend has been aimed at the bigger cities of Quebec, Ontario, or British Columbia; and much nineteenth century western settlement origi-

FIGURE 2.3: ETHNIC ORIGIN OF POPULATION, ATLANTIC PROVINCES AND CANADA, 1981

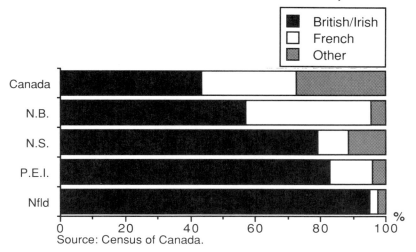

Source: Census of Canada.

nated in parts of Europe other than the British Isles or France. Nova Scotia can lay a weak claim to a slightly more diverse cultural pattern, with 11.4% of its people of non-British or non-French ancestry. These include descendants of an eighteenth century settlement of Germans along the South Shore, centred in Lunenburg County.

Language patterns in 1981 show that the overwhelming majority of Atlantic Canadians have English as their principal language at home. Even in the heavily Acadian parts of New Brunswick (the only officially bilingual province in Canada) the incidence of English as first language is higher than the proportion of New Brunswickers claiming British ancestry.

Regional Migration. For most of the twentieth century, more people have left Atlantic Canada than have come to live there. Emigration to other parts of Canada alone outweighed immigration by some 400,000 people in the sixty years between 1921 and 1981 (Table 2.2). These emigration numbers do not include substantial movements to areas such as New England (the "Boston States") where blood ties remain very strong.

The decision to leave in the first place was not always taken willingly, but was more a result of economic necessity. Economic prospects in the region during the 1970s improved, prompting a few years of positive net migration to Atlantic Canada. Many of these migrants were returning expatriates, either tempted back by the lure of work nearer home or having lost jobs as conditions deteriorated in other parts of Canada.

TABLE 2.2: NET MIGRATION BETWEEN PROVINCES IN CANADA 1921–1981

	1921–1930	1931–1940	1941–1950	1951–1960	1961–1970	1971–1980	1921–1980
	– thousands –						
Newfoundland	—	—	—	(13.0)	(34.6)	(20.8)	(68.4)
Prince Edward Island	(9.1)	(2.6)	(13.6)	(10.6)	(5.7)	2.9	(38.7)
Nova Scotia	(58.2)	4.2	(37.0)	(35.5)	(43.5)	4.2	(165.8)
New Brunswick	(33.9)	(10.8)	(40.1)	(39.3)	(45.3)	6.4	(162.5)
Quebec	55.5	(1.8)	(17.1)	198.5	(142.6)	(234.1)	(141.6)
Ontario	164.3	79.5	270.1	701.8	236.1	96.4	1355.4
Manitoba	(7.3)	(43.8)	(65.5)	(5.7)	(64.2)	(69.1)	(255.6)
Saskatchewan	15.4	(148.7)	(202.2)	(83.1)	(123.5)	(50.5)	(595.6)
Alberta	39.5	(34.5)	(15.2)	125.9	30.0	244.9	390.6
British Columbia	119.7	85.7	224.7	244.1	192.7	(214.9)	652.0

Note: Parentheses denote a net loss in population by migration.

Sources: I.B. Anderson, *Internal Migration in Canada 1921–1961*. Economic Council of Canada Staff Study No. 13, 1966; Statistics Canada Catalogue 91-210.

FIGURE 2.4: NUMBER OF PEOPLE PER ACTIVE CIVILIAN PHYSICIAN, CANADA AND PROVINCES, 1972 AND 1984

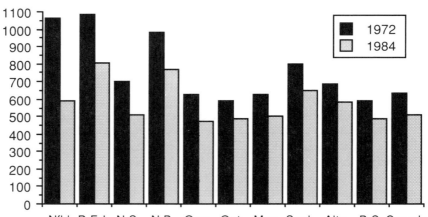

Source: Health and Welfare Canada, *Canada Health Manpower Inventory, 1985*.

Some Social Indicators

Health and Education. It is difficult to provide basic services to a dispersed and relatively rural population. Good health and education services have come to be taken for granted by Canadians, mainly because of great improvements since 1945. Atlantic Canada lags a little behind the national average in some respects, mainly because of its distribution of population. There are, for example, fewer doctors per capita in Newfoundland, Prince Edward Island, and New Brunswick than nationally, despite great improvements since the early 1970s (Figure 2.4). The presence of a substantial medical community in Halifax improves Nova Scotia's average in this respect. Similarly, there are fewer dentists; there was only one dentist for every 4,288 Newfoundlanders in 1984, compared with one for 2,001 Canadians generally.

Atlantic educational standards have improved since the mid-1970s, although there is still room for improvement. For example, about 30% of adults in Newfoundland in the 1980s have less than Grade 9 education compared with 20% nationally. Newfoundland also has the lowest proportion in Canada of its 16-year-olds enrolled in school. All the provinces have greatly improved enrolments in elementary and secondary schools, however, since the mid-1970s. Enrolment in post-secondary institutions still falls short of the national average (it is close in Nova Scotia), once again in spite of great improvements since the 1970s.

Other Indicators. Regional disparities are usually cast in economic terms, and in this respect Atlantic Canada struggles to look good. By other measures, the human condition can be demonstrated to be better than in other parts of Canada (Figure 2.5). Crime rates in the 1980s are lower than national averages, although they have shared the disturbing national tendency to increase rather rapidly. The incidence of suicide also tends to be lower, as is the divorce rate.

These indicators are broad and generally imperfect measures of "quality of life". Crime rates are influenced by effectiveness and ease of policing, for example, and divorce rates are influenced by adherence to traditional and religious values. However, the consensus, both in the region and in Canada as a whole, is that intangible social and environmental qualities make Atlantic Canada a better-than-average place to live.

FIGURE 2.5: INDICATORS OF SOCIAL STRESS, CANADA AND THE PROVINCES, 1985

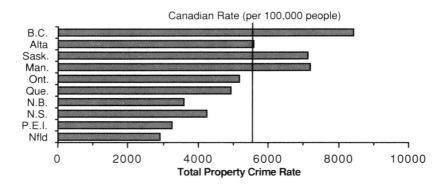

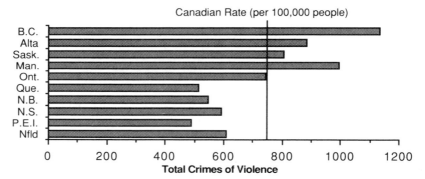

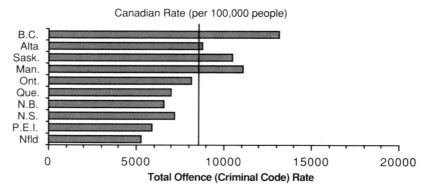

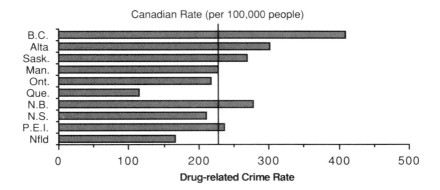

Canadian Rate (per 100,000 people)

Drug-related Crime Rate

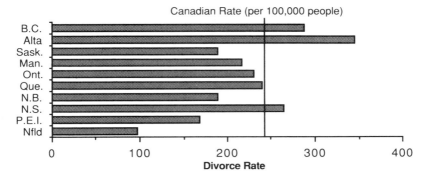

Canadian Rate (per 100,000 people)

Divorce Rate

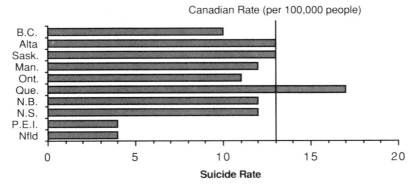

Canadian Rate (per 100,000 people)

Suicide Rate

Sources: Statistics Canada Catalogue 84-203, 84-205, and 85-205.

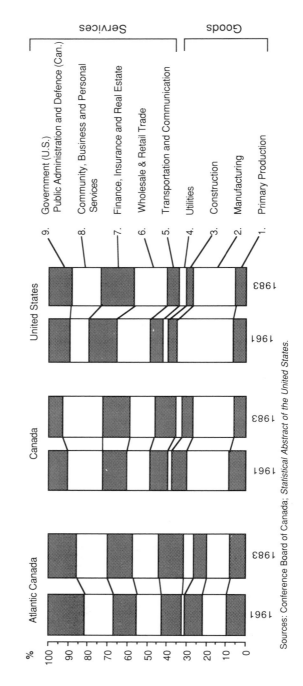

FIGURE 2.6: STRUCTURE OF GROSS DOMESTIC PRODUCT, ATLANTIC CANADA, CANADA, AND THE UNITED STATES, 1961 AND 1983

Services

Goods

9. Government (U.S.) Public Administration and Defence (Can.)
8. Community, Business and Personal Services
7. Finance, Insurance and Real Estate
6. Wholesale & Retail Trade
5. Transportation and Communication
4. Utilities
3. Construction
2. Manufacturing
1. Primary Production

United States

1983

1961

Canada

1983

1961

Atlantic Canada

1983

1961

%
100
90
80
70
60
50
40
30
20
10
0

Sources: Conference Board of Canada; *Statistical Abstract of the United States.*

22

Atlantic Canada Today

The Atlantic Economy: Basic Structure

There has been relatively little change in the basic structure of the Atlantic economy since 1961 (Figure 2.6). Service industries occupy a rather larger share of the total, with public administration and general services being the two single biggest sectors. Primary production (agriculture, fishing, forestry, and mining) gained a little ground, while manufacturing and construction both lost a little. Utilities (mostly electricity generation) tripled their share but still account for only 5% of the region's gross domestic product in the 1980s.

The regional economy differs from the national in having less manufacturing, and relatively higher dependence on direct government spending. This has been decried, but, in fact, public spending took up a smaller proportion of gross regional product in 1982 than it did in 1961. A substantial military presence in the region partly accounts for the greater importance of government spending in Atlantic Canada.

Indirectly, government spending is relatively much higher in the region than in other parts of Canada. Transfers from various levels of government to individuals in the form of pensions, unemployment insurance benefits, or direct support programs all enhance aggregate spending power; and transfers to industries in the form of incentives and grants have provided support for business.

A further comparison involves the American economy. Once again, as in Canada and Atlantic Canada, services increasingly dominate; the decline of manufacturing in the United States since the early 1960s has been striking.

Consideration of manufacturing as a part of economic structures requires an early comment. Atlantic manufacturing relies heavily on resource processing, mainly forest, agricultural and fish products. The nature of such manufacturing means there is substantially less value added by processing (per unit of output) than is the case at either Canadian or American levels, where production of items such as automobiles and computers means much more value added. Efforts to expand Atlantic Canada's higher value-added manufacturing industries have been central to regional development initiatives for several decades.

Total Atlantic gross domestic product in nominal[1] terms in 1984 was almost $26 billion, which represents an average annual increase of 10.2% since 1961 (Table 2.3). Gross domestic product per person in Atlantic Canada in 1984 was only about 65% of the national average, a modest improvement from 59% in 1961.

TABLE 2.3: GROSS DOMESTIC PRODUCT, ATLANTIC CANADA AND CANADA, 1961 AND 1984

	Atlantic Canada		Canada	
	1961	1984	1961	1984
Gross Domestic Product at Market Prices ($ billion)	2.5	25.7	40.1	490.0
Average Annual Percent Change 1961–1984	10.2%		10.5%	
Gross Domestic Product per Person (dollars)	1,310	11,212	2,202	17,375
Average Annual Percent Change 1961–1984	9.4%		9.0%	

Note: Gross *domestic* product (gdp) is not equivalent to gross *national* product (gnp), which is gdp plus the value of gross product originating outside the country in question. In the case of Canada, gdp is higher than gnp as there is a net outflow of foreign-owned product from Canada.

Source: Statistics Canada 13-213.

Attempts to improve these figures, to bring Atlantic incomes and output up to national standards, underpin most economic endeavour in the region. Discussion of some of the details of this enterprise occupies the bulk of the remainder of this book.

Footnote.

1. The expressions *real* or *constant*; and *nominal* or *current* dollars will recur frequently in this book. Nominal/current dollars are present-day values; real/constant dollars are adjusted to allow for the effects of inflation or other price changes over a given period.

Further Reading

Economic Council of Canada, *Newfoundland: From Dependency to Self-Reliance, Ottawa, 1980.* Especially chapter 1.

New Brunswick with Statistics Canada, *The Historical Statistics of New Brunswick,* 1984.

Newfoundland and Labrador, *Historical Statistics of Newfoundland and Labrador,* Volume II(2), St. John's, 1979

Prince Edward Island, *Prince Edward Island Historical Statistical Review.* Prepared by the Economics, Statistics and Fiscal Analysis Division of the Department of Finance and Tourism. Charlottetown, 1985.

Statistics Canada, *Canada Year Book: A Review of Economic, Social and Political Developments in Canada.* Ottawa, biannual.

CHAPTER 3

Agriculture:
Food and the Land

As recently as the early 1960s, Atlantic agriculture still retained significant subsistence characteristics, with small mixed farms depending on
family labour and only limited sales in localised markets. There were
some important cash crops which reached more distant markets (Annapolis Valley apples, for example, or Prince Edward Island or New
Brunswick potatoes) but Atlantic farms were primarily regarded as a
labour bank to feed growing industries elsewhere in North America.
This was a far cry from the end of the nineteenth century, when Maritime
farms helped feed a growing Canada. Before long, however, western
settlers began to cultivate the land to feed themselves and generate important exports.

For much of the twentieth century, Atlantic agriculture has been a sector
of last resort. It has absorbed labour during recession, only to see workers leave when prosperity returned. However, in the later 1960s and
1970s there was renewed vigour within agriculture, and although it remains a fairly small part of total economic activity in the region, it
retains an importance which extends beyond the farm gate. This is due
to a number of factors: the global export of commodities such as
potatoes, apples, and blueberries; the maintenance of an important processing sector; the aura of independence, honest hard work, proximity to
the earth and community values that surrounds farmers and their work.
Also, over large areas farming is an integral moulder of the landscape.

FIGURE 3.1: AREAS OF SOILS IN AGRICULTURE CAPABILITY, CLASSES 2 TO 4, ATLANTIC PROVINCES

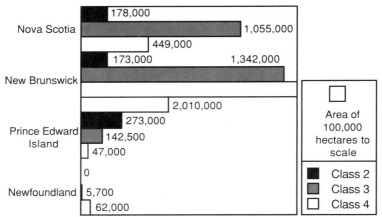

Note: The large rectangle represents the total area of the Atlantic provinces, 20.4 million hectares, excluding Labrador. The values inside the rectangle are hectares.
Source: *J.L. Nowland, The Agricultural Productivity of the Soils of the Atlantic Provinces,* Agriculture Canada, Research Branch, Monograph No. 12, 1975.

As farmers' contributions to gross regional product have declined as a share of the total, the actual volume of agricultural output and its value has increased enormously. Between 1961 and 1984, the agricultural share of the total of all goods produced in Atlantic Canada went down from 7.6% to 5%; over the same period, the actual value of receipts from the farms went up from $108 million to $718 million. As in other parts of Canada, this increase in output has been achieved by greater use of capital instead of labour; this has allowed agricultural productivity to rise dramatically over the past few decades.

Agriculture accounts for about 25% of the total value of goods produced in Prince Edward Island, while in Nova Scotia and New Brunswick it accounts for about 3%, and in Newfoundland about 1.5%.

The Land Resource[1]

There are an estimated 5.7 million hectares of land available and broadly suitable for agriculture in Atlantic Canada (Figure 3.1). This represents about one-quarter of the region's total area (excluding Labrador), but only about 607,000 hectares are classified as "prime" agricultural land (class 2). A large portion of the ultimate reserve is wooded and may be remote from established agricultural infrastructure. Many of the higher capability areas have already been cleared and improved for some kind of use.

Although the ultimate reserve seems impressive, the actual available land base is modest, taking into consideration capital inputs, location, fragmentation into relatively small pockets, and local topography. Accounting for such factors as distance to markets, cultural patterns, and extent of existing agricultural development, the realistic potential is about 2.6 million hectares. Of this total, 730,000 hectares are both in classes 2 to 4 and cleared, with the remainder under woods.

There are pockets of prime land in each province. In New Brunswick, much of the Saint John River valley is one such area, along with others around St Quentin in the north, down the east coast, and around Sussex in the south. Prime areas in Nova Scotia are in the Annapolis Valley, the northern coastal lowland from Amherst to Antigonish, around Truro down to Shubenacadie, and in Lunenburg County.

Most of Prince Edward Island, except areas in the northeast and in central Prince County, is regarded as good land. Newfoundland's only areas of mineral soils are small scattered pockets from Codroy in the west to the Avalon Peninsula in the east. Agriculture in Newfoundland is limited by poor soils and short cool summers.

About 36% of Prince Edward Island is improved farmland, which encompasses one of the biggest stretches of class 2 soils in Atlantic Canada (about one-half the improved area). The soils are generally stone-free and respond to applications of lime and fertiliser. The Island's climate is generally favourable for a wide range of crops, with some difficulties because of alternative wet and dry growing seasons. Although it is the smallest province in terms of total area, Prince Edward Island has Atlantic Canada's largest area of cleared and improved farm land.

Nova Scotia has 3.4% of its area as improved land, including most of the province's prime soils. There are some soil limitations such as bedrock near the surface, stoniness, and poor drainage. Climatic restraints include fog near the Atlantic coast, and short growing seasons that run the risk of early or late frosts.

Class 2 soils cover 2.4% of New Brunswick, and the improved area accounts for 2.6% of the province's total area. The land surface is mainly undulating, uneven, or steep, and even within areas of prime soils, farming is frequently interrupted by gullies and ridges. Soils are often podsolised (heavily leached, low in plant nutrients, and deficient in structure) with additional problems from stoniness and poor drainage. Length of growing season, defined by frost-free period, is a major limitation on occasion; otherwise a wide range of crops is possible.

Soil limitations throughout Atlantic Canada include low fertility, which requires widespread use of lime and fertiliser to correct. Cost of improvement is substantial on occasion. Undesirable soil structure and stoniness are also important limitations, and corrective steps in this respect would also entail high capital costs. This means that the margin between final commodity prices and input costs becomes a critical factor in the development of a land reserve for agriculture. The lack of much research aimed specifically at the Atlantic land resource in the past must also figure in development decisions.

Post-War Trends in Agriculture

The structure of Atlantic farming has changed dramatically since 1945. In 1951, there were 332,000 people living on about 63,700 census farms in the region; by 1981, there were only 46,590 people living on 12,941 farms.[1] Total area in farms declined from 3.2 million hectares in 1951 to 1.2 million hectares in 1981. The area of improved land dropped less severely, from 948,000 hectares (about 23% of the total area in farms) to 583,000 hectares (about 47% of the total area in farms). This proportion varied from province to province in 1981; in Prince Edward Island it was 72%, in New Brunswick, 44%, in Nova Scotia, 38%, and in Newfoundland it was 31%. The more rapid erosion of agriculture in the region compared to the nation is revealed by the fact that there was only one farm in 1981 for every five in 1951; the ratio for Canada was one to two. (See Table 3.1 for basic data.)

A 61% decline in the area of land in farms has given Atlantic Canada a label of marginal agriculture. Over substantial parts of the Maritimes, abandoned fields give substance to this impression, with shrubs and trees recolonising fields once cleared at great expense of time and labour. The demise of farming in many localities is the result of a complex array of social, economic, and physical variables. As agriculture became a highly specialised, capital-intensive industry, and as opportunities and jobs arose in other industries, emigration to towns and factories began. Usually, the more innovative people left first, anxious to improve their prospects rather than face a life of hard work for uncertain returns. Only the most determined farmers on the best land were able to survive.

The trend of rural emigration was later partly reversed when townspeople who preferred to combine an urban wage-packet with rural living began moving back to the countryside. Some of these newcomers bought land and began to raise a few animals for their own use or for limited local markets. Such agricultural enterprises, although often included in censuses, are essentially adjuncts to urban-based jobs. Some other farmers have gone the opposite way, finding an urban income to support their

TABLE 3.1: BASIC DATA FROM CENSUSES OF AGRICULTURE ATLANTIC PROVINCES AND CANADA, 1951, 1961, 1971 AND 1981

	Newfoundland and Labrador	Prince Edward Island	Nova Scotia	New Brunswick	Atlantic Canada	Canada
Farm population as % of total population:						
1951	5.5	47.6	18.0	29.1	20.5	20.8
1961	2.4	33.2	7.9	10.6	8.8	11.7
1971	1.0	19.1	3.4	4.3	3.9	6.9
1981	0.3	9.8	2.1	2.1	2.2	4.3
Number of farms:						
1951	3,626	10,137	23,515	26,431	63,709	623,091
1961	1,752	7,335	12,518	11,786	33,391	480,093
1971	1,042	4,543	6,008	5,485	17,078	366,128
1981	679	3,154	5,045	4,063	12,941	318,361
Total area in farms ('000 hectares):						
1951	34	443	1,285	1,404	3,166	70,437
1961	22	389	902	890	2,203	69,831
1971	25	314	538	542	1,419	68,665
1981	33	283	466	438	1,220	65,889
Improved area ('000 hectares):						
1951	12	261	268	407	948	39,196
1961	8	235	202	297	741	41,847
1971	8	200	156	197	561	43,768
1981	10	203	178	192	583	46,122
(as % of total area in farms):						
1951	35.3	58.9	20.9	28.9	29.9	55.6
1961	36.4	60.4	22.4	33.4	33.6	59.9
1971	32.0	63.7	29.0	36.3	39.4	63.7
1981	30.3	71.7	38.2	43.8	47.8	70.0
Average area per farm (hectares):						
1951	9.4	43.7	54.6	53.1	49.7	113.0
1961	12.6	53.0	72.1	75.5	66.0	145.5
1971	24.0	69.1	89.5	98.8	83.1	187.5
1981	48.6	89.7	92.4	107.8	94.3	207.0
Average improved area per farm (hectares):						
1951	3.3	25.7	11.4	15.4	14.9	62.9
1961	4.6	32.0	16.1	25.2	22.2	87.2
1971	7.7	44.0	26.0	35.9	32.8	119.6
1981	14.7	64.4	35.3	47.2	45.1	144.9

Source: Census of Agriculture 1951, 1961, 1971, and 1981.

agricultural operations. Such examples of part-time farming have become common in Atlantic Canada.

The true commercial farmers who managed to hang on to their land and farms had a common set of characteristics. Their farms grew, the land was used more intensively, and production was usually more specialised. Between 1961 and 1981, there was a marked increase in the number of farms over 162 hectares (400 acres) in extent (Figure 3.2). The proportion of smaller farms (less than 4 hectares or 10 acres) also increased, reflecting the increase in part-time farming. The proportion of mid-sized farms declined. The increase of part-time farming explains why farm population in Nova Scotia, New Brunswick and Newfoundland has increased since 1971.

Average area of land in farms between 1961 and 1981 went up from 12.5 hectares to 49 hectares in Newfoundland; from 53 hectares to 90 hectares in Prince Edward Island; from 72 hectares to 92 hectares in Nova Scotia; and from 76 hectares to 108 hectares in New Brunswick.

Capital investment increased in line with size of farms. Total capital value in Atlantic farms in 1961 was about $411 million (divided in the

FIGURE 3.2: FARMS CLASSIFIED BY AREA, ATLANTIC CANADA, 1961 AND 1981

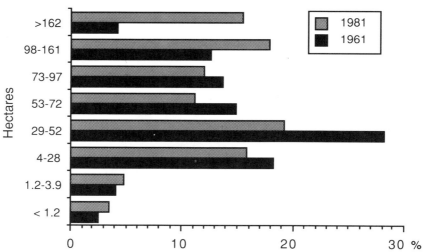

Note: All censuses before 1976 compile area data in acres, and the size classes in this figure reflect direct conversion to hectares. One hectare equals 2.471 acres.
Source: Census of Agriculture 1961 and 1981.

Atlantic Canada Today

census between land and buildings, and livestock and poultry); the figure in 1981 was $2.4 billion, an increase of 484% in nominal terms. Average capital value per Atlantic farm went up from $12,309 to $46,506 in real terms, or by 6.9% each year on average. Much of this increase can be attributed directly to appreciation in rural land values over the two decades.

Farm capital values in Atlantic Canada remain much lower than the national average (Figure 3.3). In 1981, farms in Prince Edward Island were the most highly capitalised in the region (about $222,000 on average); this compared with a national average of $409,000, and with $634,000 in Alberta. Much of the differential lies in varying values placed on farm land. Much western and Ontario farmland is better quality than in the Atlantic region and supports higher value crops, such as wheat for export or intensively cultivated fruit. It is natural, therefore, that crop values and inherent quality should be capitalised into land values. A further element involves competition for land, with much farmland being under severe pressure from urban development in various parts of Canada. Several of Atlantic Canada's biggest cities (Halifax, St. John's and Saint John) were founded around their harbours, and are not near enough to farmland to pose much threat of urbanisation.

These figures for capital values refer to 1981. Since then, a period of great difficulty for farmers has seen value of land decline in line with commodity prices. High interest rates in the early part of the decade forced many farmers into bankruptcy. Those in Atlantic Canada, because of lower levels of capitalisation, were largely able to escape loss of their farms while not entirely avoiding problems generally.

FIGURE 3.3: AVERAGE CAPITAL VALUES PER FARM, CANADA AND THE PROVINCES, 1981

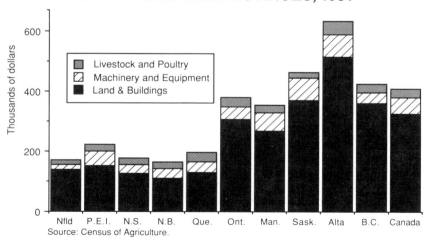

Source: Census of Agriculture.

Major Commodity and Farm Income Trends

The smaller mixed farms that characterised Atlantic agriculture in the 1950s and early 1960s have largely given way to more specialised units of production. Dairying, in particular, has become important in the Maritime provinces (Table 3.2). Apparent concentrations of cattle on farms (between 20% and 30% of commercial farms in the Maritimes) are misleading. The average number of cattle per farm is low, there are very few large feedlots in the region, and the definition of a "commercial" farm in the census is set to capture many small, part-time operations.

Proportions of hog farms, however, probably understate the importance and growth of hog production in recent years. Average number of animals per farm in Newfoundland and Nova Scotia exceeds the national average. The fact that there are fewer farms reporting a majority of their receipts from hog sales means that such operations are big, specialised, capital-intensive units rearing many hundreds of animals at once. Commercial marketings of hogs within the region have increased markedly since the mid-1960s.

A concentration of farms producing field crops in New Brunswick and Prince Edward Island reflects potato growing (Table 3.2). A degree of fruit and vegetable specialisation in Nova Scotia is due to the Annapolis Valley's apple orchards, blueberries in the north of the province, and scattered vegetable production. Newfoundland's relatively large degree of fruit and vegetable specialisation is in response to local demand for fresh produce in a market at the very end of North American supply lines. Tobacco is grown in the Maritime provinces, usually in areas with longer, more reliable frost-free periods; the biggest area is in Prince Edward Island.

Farm cash receipts in the Maritime provinces increased from $112.3 million in 1960-1962 (three-year average) to $150.2 million in 1983-1985 in terms of 1961 dollars (Table 3.3). Dairy products and potatoes are the two dominant components, although cattle and calf receipts were relatively more important in the early 1960s. Hog receipts have also increased in relative importance. The biggest increases in receipts have occurred for fruits and vegetables (up 91%), hogs (up 91%), dairy products (up 80%), and potatoes (up 41%).

Commodity mix varies from province to province. In Newfoundland, where cash receipts amounted to $43 million in 1983-1985, almost half this total came from poultry and eggs, with a further 32% from dairy products and hogs. About 31% of receipts in Prince Edward Island came

TABLE 3.2: PERCENTAGE DISTRIBUTION OF COMMERCIAL FARMS [1] CLASSIFIED BY PRODUCT TYPE [2] FOR THE ATLANTIC PROVINCES, 1981

Product Type	Newfoundland and Labrador	Prince Edward Island	Nova Scotia	New Brunswick
	\- percent of total \-			
Dairy	15.1	29.7	26.2	27.1
Cattle	8.8	21.2	29.8	26.8
Hogs	6.7	9.8	6.2	4.3
Poultry	13.8	1.0	4.0	3.7
Wheat	—	0.2	0.3	0.3
Small grains (excluding wheat)	—	3.3	1.5	1.7
Field crops other than small grains	5.2	17.9	2.3	16.2
Fruits and vegetables	22.7	2.0	14.2	8.5
Miscellaneous special	13.7	3.4	10.1	6.1
Mixed farms	14.3	11.4	5.3	5.1
Livestock combination	2.6	7.9	2.9	2.6
Field crops combination	0.2	1.8	0.3	0.8
Other combination	11.5	1.9	2.1	1.6

Note: 1) A commercial farm is defined as having sales of $2,500 or more
2) Product type is defined as a farm selling at least 50% of its total output as that product.

Source: Census of Agriculture 1981.

from potatoes in 1984, although this proportion has varied widely from year to year; in 1979, for example, potatoes were only 24% of total receipts, but were as high as 42% in 1974. All livestock (including dairy, beef and hogs) accounted for 45% of receipts.

Nova Scotia has the highest level of receipts in the region, with rather less dependence on only one or two products. Dairy products are the most important, followed by poultry and eggs, cattle and calves, hogs, and fruit and vegetables. New Brunswick relies mainly on potatoes, dairying, other livestock, with some grains and fruits.

TABLE 3:3: FARM CASH RECEIPTS, MARITIME PROVINCES, 1961–1963 AND 1983–1985 [1]

	1961–1963[2]		1982–1984[2,3]		Annual Average Change
	$'000	%	$'000	%	%
Dairy products	19,130	17.0	34,446	23.0	2.7
Poultry and eggs	17,781	15.8	19,419	12.9	0.4
Hogs	9,438	8.4	16,822	11.2	2.7
Cattle and calves	18,505	16.5	16,277	10.8	–0.6
Potatoes	19,037	17.0	26,890	17.9	1.6
Fruits and vegetables	7,643	6.8	14,578	9.7	3.0
Other receipts	20,723	18.4	21,717	14.5	0.2
Total receipts	112,257	100.0	150,169	100.0	1.3

Notes: 1) No data exist for the earlier period for Newfoundland. The 1961 census of agriculture revealed total sales worth $4.3 million in 1960. Farm cash receipts in 1985 (in 1961 dollars) were $10 million.

2) Data for the two periods are the averages over three years.

3) Dollar values for 1983–85 are in terms of 1961 dollars, weighted by the Farm Input Price Index for eastern Canada.

Source: Statistics Canada 21-001.

Agriculture: Some Characteristics

Good Years and Bad. In a world economy dominated by huge corporations and market rigidities, agriculture is rather unusual. Its primary production comes from a large number of small producers each of whom has no real influence over the markets in which he sells. He is a price-taker rather than a price-maker. The supply of agricultural products is such that small variations in the total amount produced for markets result in proportionally greater variations in prices received. The result is often a paradox; for example, good harvests will depress prices, while poor harvests increase them.

This simplified characterisation of agricultural production is complicated by many things. These include stockpiles of products, regulations, crop and herd successes around the world, and premiums commanded by local production because of freshness or reputation. Another thing is that reliance on a limited range of production, such as potato production in Prince Edward Island and New Brunswick, involves more vulnerability in the face of year-to-year swings in output and prices. Where farming underpins a much wider range of economic activity (supplying inputs, veterinary services, trucking, food processing, and so on) such vulnerability affects more than agriculture itself.

Agricultural Specialisation. As farmers have become more commercial and specialised they have become less self-reliant. For example, formerly winter fodder for livestock was grown on the farm and fertilised by manure from the stock barns; now, in the mid-1980s, both fodder and fertiliser are brought in.

Increased specialisation at the farm level arouses mixed emotions. On the one hand, farmers must achieve economies of scale to survive and expand their businesses. On the other hand, North American agriculture is solidly based on the family farm as the main unit of production. The rural values embodied in this reality have been a potent force in moulding discussion of agricultural change, although it is doubtful whether they have actually deterred such change.

The Cost-Price Squeeze. Over the past decade, the farmer has become vulnerable to a phenomenon termed the cost-price squeeze. Exercising minimal influence over prices received, he is at the mercy of cost increases. This was particularly so during the high-inflation, high-cost period of the 1970s and early 1980s. Total agricultural expenses in the Maritimes increased by an average of 12% a year between 1970 and 1980; consumer food prices went up by 10% a year. The cost of energy (also affecting items that require relatively high amounts of energy in

TABLE 3.4: FARM OPERATING EXPENSES, ATLANTIC PROVINCES AND CANADA, 1983

	Newfoundland and Labrador	Prince Edward Island	Nova Scotia	New Brunswick	Canada
Total Operating Expenses ($ million)	26.4	118.7	175.2	141.1	12,925.1
			– percent of total –		
Taxes	0.1	1.2	1.1	1.5	2.1
Gross farm rent	0.4	2.5	0.9	0.7	5.4
Wages to farm labour	14.9	13.9	15.8	13.5	9.6
Interest	5.6	11.3	8.0	11.9	14.7
Total machinery expenses	8.2	18.3	13.1	17.9	18.3
Fertiliser and lime	3.9	12.9	4.3	8.7	9.4
Other crop expenses	3.0	8.8	4.7	7.2	7.9
Feed	50.0	14.5	38.2	26.4	15.1
Other livestock expenses	2.7	4.3	2.4	1.5	4.5
Repairs to buildings	1.6	2.2	2.4	2.4	2.0
Electricity and telephone	3.1	3.2	3.0	3.2	2.6
Miscellaneous	6.5	6.9	6.1	5.0	8.3

Source: Agriculture Canada, *Market Commentary, Proceedings of the Canadian Agriculture Outlook Conference,* December 1984.

their manufacture, such as fertiliser) went up by as much as five times over the decade. High interest rates meant high carrying costs on debt, both for capital projects and operating costs such as the classic "seedtime to harvest" borrowing.

Maritime farmers have done reasonably well during the period of high costs, in comparison with farmers nationally; costs in Canada went up by an average of 15% between 1970 and 1980. Cost structures reflect provincial emphasis on production (Table 3.4). Feed costs are relatively more important in Nova Scotia and Newfoundland, where dairying and hogs are also important. Crop-related expenses figure larger in Prince Edward Island and New Brunswick. Interest costs in general assume less importance than nationally, probably because Atlantic agriculture is less capitalised.

Regulation of Agriculture. Limited market influence by individual farmers has been offset by the establishment of marketing boards (Table 3.5). These regulate year-to-year fluctuations in returns caused by circumstances beyond farmers' influence caused by market or natural forces. This form of agricultural regulation affects substantial proportions of receipts and incomes, and is the subject of constant discussion; should the power of the boards over commodities already covered be extended, or should new boards be created? Although all marketing boards are privately administered, public bodies oversee their operations and set rules. Variations (between provinces, and commodities)in the way these

TABLE 3.5: MARKETING BOARD STATISTICS, ATLANTIC PROVINCES 1984/1985

	Newfoundland and Labrador	Prince Edward Island	Nova Scotia	New Brunswick
Number of boards	5	6	10	15
Number of producers affected	247	2,483	1,972	8,597
Proportion of total receipts affected	80%	65%	61%	66%
Commodities covered	Broilers	Potatoes	Winter grain	Apples
	Eggs	Pedigreed	Processing	Potatoes
	Vegetables	seed [1]	peas	Greenhouse
	Hogs	Tobacco	Tobacco	plants
	Dairy	Hogs	Dairy	Dairy
	products	Dairy	products	products
		products	Broilers	Broilers
		Broilers	Turkeys	Turkeys
		Eggs	Eggs and	Eggs
			pullets	Wood
			Wool	Cattle [1]
			Potatoes	Hogs
			Hogs	

Note: 1) Educational and promotional only.

Source: Agriculture Canada, *Marketing Board Statistics, Canada 1984–85*, Marketing and Economic Branch (Co-operatives Unit). Compiled by J.M. Sullivan.

boards apply their powers reflect the wishes of producers, a majority of whom must vote for a marketing board before it is established. Most farmers in Atlantic Canada are under some form of regulation, but they appear to view this as a necessary evil. Boards have been criticised on the basis that they cost too much to run; that they do not notably affect an imbalance of marketing influence that strongly favours concentrated processing and distribution industries; and that they erode producer independence. Consumers perceive the effects of such boards as artificially high prices at the same time as expensive stockpiles accumulate.

Defenders of regulation, in turn, argue that in the absence of boards there would be destructive competition in an industry such as agriculture; that individual farmers do not have adequate access to market information; that in the absence of boards returns to farm families would be too low to sustain a reasonable lifestyle; that regional policy in Canada requires a degree of agricultural support to ensure some economic viability; and that a capacity for full self-reliance in food production in Canada is an implicit national goal.

Research and Extension. Government involvement in agriculture also takes in research and extension roles. Farmers individually have little time and few resources to engage in activities such as plant and animal breeding, soils research, and so on. Much of this work is either undertaken by corporations that supply inputs to the industry, or by federal and provincial governments. Federal efforts are especially important in research and development, with experimental stations across Canada, including six in the Atlantic region. Provincial governments also engage in research and are particularly responsible for delivering new innovations to farmers by means of extension services.

Agriculture Canada alone spent almost $21 million on research in 1982/1983 in Atlantic Canada, or about 29% of all of the department's spending in the region in that fiscal year; some $181 million was spent nationally on research. Other programs to encourage agricultural development have been run by other federal departments such as the Department of Regional Industrial Expansion, usually with the support of the provinces.

Agricultural Processing

The work of Atlantic farmers extends beyond the farm gate. An important part of Atlantic manufacturing deals with processing agricultural products, and this has become a highly sophisticated industry. As in fishing, there are important linkages to local resources, but unlike fish processors, agricultural processors do not rely to the same extent on local supplies of raw materials; bakeries, for example, will draw on supplies of western grain. The industry has become quite concentrated in some respects, as in fruit and vegetable processing in western New Brunswick and Prince Edward Island. In some cases export markets have been developed to supplement a heavy reliance on localised sales.

Principal components are dairies, meat-packing plants, bakeries, and fruit and vegetable processors. The region's dairies are substantially limited by quota systems to supplying intra-provincial markets only with fluid milk, although some other dairy products receive wider distribution. The 1984 census of manufacturing identified about 12,000 jobs in agricultural processing, with some seasonality to employment patterns. Related industries include breweries.

A degree of concentration in the processing industry may see farmers bearing the extra costs of shipping products over longer distances to market, and may further erode their market power when confronted with relatively few and big buyers. This, in turn, tends to foster further concentration of agriculture, larger farms, and encourages cooperation among farmers to bargain for contracts and prices.

Summary

The farming industry in Atlantic Canada has wide-ranging linkages to other sectors and underpins most important sub-provincial economies in parts of the Maritime provinces. Development of the sector since 1945 has been on a smaller scale than nationally, and has been aimed more at supplying regional markets rather than for export. Some important export markets have been penetrated for certain products.

The balance of the century will be a trying time for all farmers in the industrialised world, since high levels of national regulation, subsidy, and protection have resulted in considerable surpluses around the world. Painful adjustment has already begun, and this will not bypass Atlantic Canada. There is little doubt, however, that the region's farmers are in a better competitive position than ever before to meet new challenges, both in supplying regional markets with good food at reasonable prices, and in exploring new export directions.

Footnotes

1. This section draws on information in J.L. Nowland, *The Agricultural Productivity of the Soils of the Atlantic Provinces*, Agriculture Canada, Soil Research Institute, Monograph No. 12, Ottawa, 1975. See also J.R. Hilchey, *Soil Capability Analysis for Agriculture in Nova Scotia*, Department of Regional Economic Expansion, Canada Land Inventory, Report No. 8, Ottawa, 1970.

   Agricultural Capability Classes are devised by the Canada Land Inventory. The classification ranges from class 1 (highest capability for agriculture) to class 7 (no capability for agriculture). Most of Canada's class 1 soils are in southern Ontario, and land reserves for agriculture in Atlantic Canada are largely confined to classes 2, 3, and 4, which have limitations ranging from moderate to severe for growing crops. In general, crops can be grown with reasonable assurance on class 2 soils and some class 3. Most class 3 and 4 soils are more suitable for pasture.

2. The definition of a census farm has varied over the years. In 1951 it was defined as a holding "on which agricultural operations are carried out"; it must be at least three acres or more in size, or less than this but with agricultural production valued at $250 or more in 1950. In 1981, the definition of a census farm was one with sales of agricultural products in the previous 12 months (up to day of the census) of $250 or more. Commercial farms are vastly bigger than this. Initial results from the 1986 census of agriculture were issued as this book went to the publisher. These revealed that there were $11,321 census farms in Atlantic Canada in that year, a drop of 12.5%. Total area in census farms was a little over 1.1 million hectares, down by 7% from 1981. The biggest apparent losses were in Nova Scotia and New Brunswick, although it is uncertain how much is accounted for by part-time operations.

Further Reading

Abramson, J.A., *Rural to Urban Adjustment*. ARDA Research Report No. RE-4, Ministry of Forestry and Rural Development, Ottawa, 1968.

Agriculture Canada, *Handbook of Selected Agricultural Statistics*. Regional Development Branch, Ottawa, annual.

Agriculture Canada, *The Orientation of Canadian Agriculture: A Task Force Report*. Three volumes, Ottawa, 1977.

Atlantic Development Board, *The Competitive Position of Maritime Agriculture*. Background Report No. 2, Ottawa, 1969. Especially Chapters 3 to 5.

Brinkman, G.E., *Farm Incomes in Canada*. Prepared for the Economic Council of Canada and the Institute for Research on Public Policy, Ottawa, 1981.

Economic Council of Canada, *Reforming Regulation*. Ottawa, 1981. Chapter 6.

Kennedy, P. and M. Churches, *Canada's Agricultural Systems*. Fourth edition, Department of Agricultural Economics, Macdonald Campus of McGill University, Ste Anne de Bellevue, 1981.

New Brunswick, *Report of the Agricultural Resources Study*. A.C. Parks, Executive Director, Fredericton, 1977.

Nowland, J.L., *The Agricultural Productivity of the Soils of the Atlantic Provinces*. Agriculture Canada, Soil Research Institute, Monograph No. 12, Ottawa, 1975.

Pepin, P-Y, *Life and Poverty in the Maritimes*. ARDA Research Report No. RE-3, Ministry of Forestry and Rural Development, Ottawa, 1968.

Senate of Canada, *Soil at Risk: Canada's Eroding Future*. A Report by the Standing Senate Committee on Agriculture, Fisheries and Forestry, Hon. Herbert O. Sparrow, Chairman, Ottawa, 1984.

Simpson-Lewis, W. *et al., Canada's Special Resource Lands: A National Perspective of Selected Land Uses*. Lands Directorate, Environment Canada, Map Folio No. 4, Ottawa, 1979. Especially Section 1.

Statistics Canada, *A Profile of Canadian Agriculture*. 1981 Census of Agriculture, Ottawa, 1984.

CHAPTER 4

The Fishery: A Resource and its Promise

The sea and fishing are the essence of Atlantic Canada. The fishery attracted the first European settlers, when Portuguese, Breton, and English fishermen used Newfoundland as a base to dry cod caught on the Banks. German farmers on Nova Scotia's South Shore turned with equal facility to fishing, as did many other settlers in other parts. They built a reputation for seamanship and shipbuilding which stands today.

Fishing represents the lifeblood of more than 1,300 small communities in the region and a cornerstone of industry. It dominates economic activity outside big urban areas, and influences the social fabric of many coastal rural areas. The Task Force on Atlantic Fisheries [1] estimated conservatively in 1982 that 62,250 jobs in both harvesting and processing fish are in these communities, which have usually less than 500 inhabitants and comprise 25% of the Atlantic population. Table 4.1 outlines the relative importance of the fishery in each province in 1981.

The industry is usually considered in two parts: harvesting (or catching the fish) and processing, which also includes marketing. However, some large integrated companies are involved in all aspects of the fishery. Many people still regard the small independent fisherman, selling either to processing companies or directly to the consumer, as typical of the industry.

TABLE 4.1: RELATIVE IMPORTANCE OF THE FISHING INDUSTRY IN THE ATLANTIC PROVINCES, 1981

	Newfoundland and Labrador	Prince Edward Island	Nova Scotia	New Brunswick
		– percent –		
Contribution to value— added in commodity— producing industries	16	14	17	6
Fishermen and plant workers as proportion of employment in com- modity—producing industries	55	29	17	12

Source: Task Force on Atlantic Fisheries, *Navigating Troubled Waters: A New Policy for the Atlantic Fisheries.* Report of the Task Force on Atlantic Fisheries, M.J.L. Kirby, Chairman, 1982.

FIGURE 4.1: NOMINAL CATCHES OF ALL SPECIES IN THE NORTHWEST ATLANTIC, 1966–1984[1]

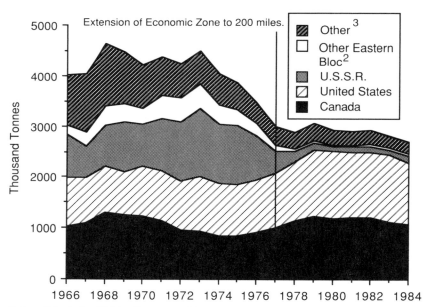

Notes: 1) Includes Fishing Zones 0-6. Much of Zones 0-4 are in Canadian waters except Zone 1 (off Greenland).
2) Bulgaria, Cuba, German Democratic Republic, Poland and Rumania.
3) Denmark, Faeroe Islands, Federal Republic of Germany, France, Iceland, Italy, Japan, Norway, Portugal, Spain, United Kingdom and unspecified.

Source: Northwest Atlantic Fisheries Organization,*Statistical Bulletin* Vol: 34, 1986.

The Resource and Two Decades of Change

Some 1.4 million tonnes of seafish were landed in Canada in 1986, of which some 80% were landed at Atlantic ports (excluding Quebec). The value of this catch to fishermen was almost $750 million. Processing on shore increased this value greatly; Atlantic exports of fish and fish products alone were worth $1.6 billion dollars in 1986, representing 65% of the Canadian total. Canada is the world's most important fish-exporting country (up from third as recently as 1976) although it ranks only 16th in terms of total catch, accounting for about 2% of the global total in recent years.

The northwest Atlantic has long attracted heavy international fishing effort, mostly on the Banks that rise from the continental shelf and provide ideal habitat for a range of species. Canada is only one country that fishes in this rich area, and our share of the catch has increased from about 25% in 1966 to about 40% in 1984 (Figure 4.1). The actual amount of fish taken by Canadian vessels has stayed fairly constant, and the increased share of the total has been achieved as the total itself has come down. Most of the effort comes now from Canadian and American fleets. Fishing by foreign fleets has been sharply reduced; catches by Soviet boats especially have come down since the early 1970s, a time when they caught more fish than either Canadian or American fleets.

Both the United States and Canada have extended their jurisdiction over the fishery to 200 nautical miles (about 370 km). The Canadian extension occurred in 1977, to take in most, but not all, of the best fishing grounds on the Banks. Progressive reduction of foreign effort, in fact, began in 1964, when a nine-mile limit was declared. This came after years of negotiations through the International Commission for the Northwest Atlantic Fisheries (now the Northwest Atlantic Fisheries Organization), which was established in 1949. The Gulf of St Lawrence became an exclusive zone in 1970, but landings continued to fall. A low point was reached in 1974, when Canadian landings were only 418,000 tonnes from the Canadian zone (roughly NAFO zones 0, 2, 3, and 4).

These severe declines in catches led to lengthy negotiations which preceded declaration of the 200-mile limit. The eventual cooperation of most fishing nations came after a series of bilateral agreements that gave foreign vessels access to stocks deemed surplus to Canadian needs. This saw almost immediate results. Canadian catches recovered. As the dollar lost value exports increased, pushing Canada to world leadership in 1978.

The most valuable exports are shellfish, including lobster, scallops, and

TABLE 4.2: VALUE AND VARIETY OF FISH EXPORTS FROM ATLANTIC CANADA AND CANADA, 1986

	Atlantic Canada	Canada	Atlantic as Proportion of Canada
	– $'000 –		– % –
Shellfish	485,046	589,502	82.4
Frozen, filleted fish	302,626	361,019	83.8
Fresh fish or frozen fish blocks nes [1]	196,089	215,313	91.1
Salted and/or dried fish	128,395	145,686	88.1
Filleted fresh or chilled fish	128,107	172,997	74.1
Whole or dressed fresh fish	97,875	150,446	65.1
Whole or dressed frozen fish	80,756	351,042	23.0
Other fish or feed nes [1]	61,175	176,543	34.6
Canned fish	41,444	191,501	21.6
Pickled fish	22,013	23,834	92.4
Smoked, or salted and smoked fish	11,838	18,996	62.3
Totals	1,555,364	2,396,879	64.9

Note: 1) Not elsewhere specified. These are Statistics Canada's Trade of Canada categories.

Source: Statistics Canada, Special Tabulations.

crabs (Table 4.2). A large part of all exports go to American markets in the form of fish blocks, which are processed into consumer products in US plants. A large part of value-added to an important Atlantic resource is lost, therefore, to a foreign economy.

Although each of the four provinces relies on a limited number of species, the degree of this reliance has varied over time. This reflects both stocks and markets, as well as local variations in the nature of the fishery. Cod has been the principal species in Newfoundland for many years, accounting for 53% of landed values in 1986 (Table 4.3 and Figure 4.2a). Other important species are flatfish, lobster, and shrimp. Capelin have assumed a place second only to cod in 1986 after a rapid rise. This is a roe (fish egg) fishery, mildly controversial because of the waste involved; only female fish carry roe and all the males and a large proportion of female carcasses have no market.

Much of the cod volume is taken by traps near the shore, with some large vessels fishing offshore. One of the "ghosts" in the Newfoundland fishery is squid, which was second only to cod in 1979 as markets beckoned, with landed values exceeding $19 million; a mere 1 tonne of squid was recorded as landed in 1986.

TABLE 4.3: VALUES OF LANDINGS BY PRINCIPAL SPECIES GROUPS AND PROVINCE, 1979 AND 1986

	Newfoundland and Labrador		Prince Edward Island		Nova Scotia		New Brunswick	
	1979	1986	1979	1986	1979	1986	1979	1986
	—millions of dollars—							
Groundfish	97.3	137.1	4.3	6.2	80.2	175.4	6.7	10.8
Pelagic	20.4	29.7	1.9	3.1	22.3	24.4	18.8	14.5
Shellfish	41.6	29.3	23.2	41.0	122.9	208.0	28.1	68.8
Total	159.3	196.1	29.4	50.3	225.5	407.8	53.6	94.1

Note: Groundfish species, which include cod, haddock, flounder, and hake, live and feed at or near the bottom of the sea. Pelagic species, which include herring, capelin, mackerel, salmon and tuna, have a wider vertical feeding range in the sea. Shellfish either have an external shell (lobster and crabs); an internal shell (squid); or live in a shell (scallops, mussels, clams and oysters). There is a small component of "other" species in the shellfish total, mostly marine plants such as Irish moss or dulse.

Source: Department of Fisheries and Oceans. Data for 1986 are subject to revision.

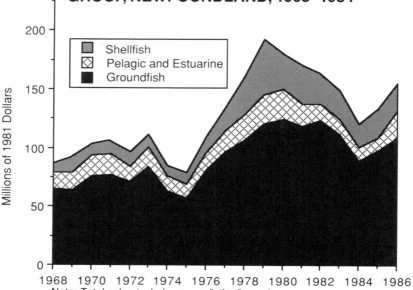

FIGURE 4.2A: LANDED VALUES BY MAIN SPECIES GROUP, NEWFOUNDLAND, 1968–1984

Note: Total value includes some "other" species.
Source: Department of Fisheries and Oceans.

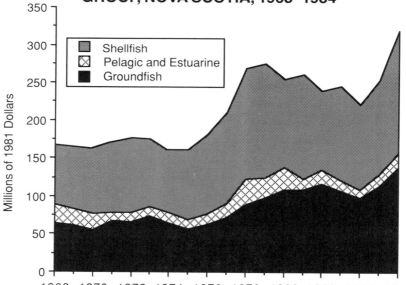

FIGURE 4.2B: LANDED VALUES BY MAIN SPECIES GROUP, NOVA SCOTIA, 1968–1984

Note: Total value includes some "other" species.
Source: Department of Fisheries and Oceans.

FIGURE 4.2C: LANDED VALUES BY MAIN SPECIES GROUP, PRINCE EDWARD ISLAND 1968–1984

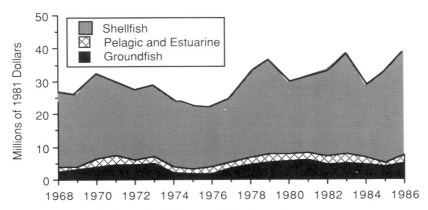

Note: Total value includes some "other" species.

Source: Department of Fisheries and Oceans.

FIGURE 4.2D: LANDED VALUES BY MAIN SPECIES GROUP, NEW BRUNSWICK, 1968–1984

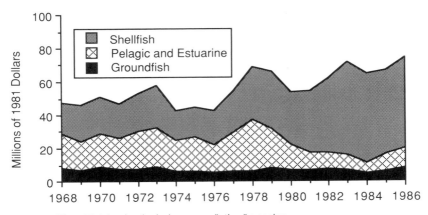

Note: Total value includes some "other" species.

Source: Department of Fisheries and Oceans.

Nova Scotia has three fairly stable species (lobster, cod, and scallops) and a more varied fishery than any other of the provinces (Figure 4.2b). There is a large offshore fleet (including Canada's first factory freezer trawler), a sophisticated midshore fleet (seiners and draggers) and an extensive inshore fishery. Lobster was the most valuable species in 1986 (landings worth $134 million) followed by cod and scallops. These three combined to account for 68% of the province's landed values of $408 million in 1986. Other important species are haddock and other groundfish species, and herring. This last, once again, has become a roe fishery in the 1980s. The Nova Scotia fishery also has its ghosts. Squid worth $10 million were landed in 1979, and swordfish worth almost $9 million. Landings for both species in 1986 were virtually non-existent.

Lobster has formed an increasing share of the Prince Edward Island fishery since the mid-1970s, and landings worth $36 million in 1986 were 72% of all landings (Figure 4.2c). The Island's fishery is overwhelmingly an inshore effort depending on small boats. A special aspect is the bluefin tuna fishery. These fish can weigh up to several hundred kilograms. It is largely a rod and line fishery with a ready market for fresh fish airlifted to distant places such as Japan; and its value exceeds landings, as many of the fish are caught by tourists who charter boats, with the owner retaining selling rights over any fish taken.

The single most valuable species in New Brunswick in 1986 was lobster, closely followed by queen crab; values for each were $29 million and $26 million respectively (Figure 4.2d). Fishing for crab is a recent development in the Gulf, taking advantage of strong North American markets and collapse of the Alaska king crab fishery in the late 1970s.

It is evident, therefore, that the composition of catches varies widely over short periods. Reasons for this are environmental, biological, and market-related. An example is herring. Up to the early 1970s, the herring caught in Atlantic Canada were used overwhelmingly for fish meal and oil. Then North Sea herring stocks collapsed because of overfishing, and the Canadian fishery found itself with a large and valuable market in Europe for herring as food. Prices jumped from $60 to $300 a tonne almost overnight. Fishermen built and equipped very sophisticated boats, and processors abandoned oil and meal reduction plants for ones to manufacture food from herring.

The North Sea stocks recovered, and in the 1980s European markets were supplied locally without buying from Canada. Fishermen and processors found it hard to return to lower-value sales of meal and oil. Some alternatives have been found, including "over-the-side" sales directly to foreign vessels, and the roe fishery. Both are controversial to a degree, the first because no shore-based processing jobs are created, the second because of generated waste and disposal problems.

The Fishermen

There were about 50,000 registered fishermen in Atlantic Canada in 1983, split between full-time and part-time. Although this is down from almost 55,000 in 1980, it is far above levels of the early 1970s. In 1974, for example, there were fewer than 31,000 fishermen registered. The increase since then was largely due to a wave of optimism after extending jurisdiction in 1977, and much of the increase was in Newfoundland, where numbers increased from less than 13,000 in 1974 to more than 35,000 in 1980. The total in Newfoundland has since slipped back to about 28,000.

Being a registered fisherman doesn't necessarily mean you fish, nor that you earn the majority of your income from fishing. Members of trawler crews may hold licences, many fishermen may hold licences for more than one species. The Task Force recorded a total of almost 28,000 bona fide fishermen out of 48,434 to whom licences were issued in 1981.

Fishing is a highly seasonal occupation, even for a full-time fisherman. The Task Force found that 75% of fishermen worked fewer than 30 weeks each year. Full-time fishermen averaged 23.1 weeks of work fishing, while part-timers averaged only 11.8 weeks. Incomes reflect these patterns, although in practice full-time fishermen earn four times the incomes of part-timers. This is mostly due to the larger number of licences for profitable species (such as scallops) held by full-timers.

The Task Force estimated full-time fishermen earned an average before-tax net income of $15,791 in 1981, from all sources; this included $2,466 (16%) from unemployment benefits, and $927 (6%) from other work. Part-time fishermen earned an average of $11,182 including $1,483 from transfers and a hefty $6,203 from other employment.

Fully 40% of full-time fishermen's households in 1981 had an average income below the official poverty line (set at $12,035 for a four-person household). This rather startling revelation affects different areas of each province with different intensity. It also introduces one of the paradoxes of the fishery. Few people dispute the wealth of the resource, even though this may vary over time. But relatively few fishermen can sustain high incomes for more than a few years at a time, and most of them are trapped in a low-income, low-skill, low-equity spiral. This is aggravated in a region where alternative economic opportunities are relatively scarce, a factor which must be considered when policies to reduce numbers of fishermen are discussed.

The Fishing Fleet

There were 27,094 registered fishing vessels in 1983 in Atlantic Canada. The majority of these were in Newfoundland (61% of the total) and Nova Scotia (23%). The number of vessels increased by 35% between 1976 and 1980 (Figure 4.3). As with increases in numbers of fishermen over this period, much of this is due to explosive growth in the New-foundland fleet, which doubled in size over the period. The total number of vessels in the other provinces actually declined at the same time.

Vessels over 100 feet long (mostly side and stern trawlers, and scallop draggers) account for the majority of landings. The 150-foot side and stern trawlers, for example, accounted for 43% of groundfish landings in 1981. Offshore vessels (over 100 feet long) are owned by a few large processors. The 18,000 or so inshore and midshore vessels are owner-operated.

Most smaller inshore vessels are in Newfoundland (Figure 4.3). This province has a large nearshore trap fishery, which saw a great expansion of effort between 1977 and 1980; numbers of boats went from less than 10,000 to more than 19,000, mostly less than 10 tonnes. Many of the variations in the size of the fleet are due to expansion and contraction in the numbers of small boats that actually participate in the fishery.

Much of the offshore effort is in Nova Scotia, although fish may be taken in waters off other provinces. The inshore fishery is characterised by a multi-species effort in which lobster plays a leading role. New Brunswick's main effort is in the Gulf of St Lawrence, with some in the Bay of Fundy and Gulf of Maine. Fishermen in Prince Edward Island are heavily specialised in lobster fishing with licences for other species outside lobster seasons. Unlike the experience of Newfoundland since 1977, the smallest inshore boats in the Maritimes have steadily given way to larger, more advanced vessels.

The diversity of vessels is supplemented by the number of harvesting techniques practised. Fish can be caught in fixed traps, weirs, gill nets, purse seine nets, trawls, by dragging, by lines, or by other means. The vessels used can range in size from dories with small outboards to factory and freezer ships equipped with the latest electronic finding and navigation gadgets.

FIGURE 4.3: NUMBER OF REGISTERED FISHING VESSELS, ATLANTIC PROVINCES, 1973–1983

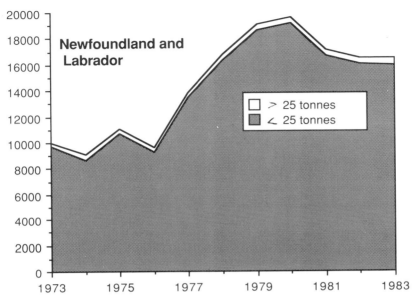

Note: Most vessels 25 tonnes or less are inshore boats. There are no data for the Maritime Provinces for 1977. There are only a few boats 26 tonnes or more in Prince Edward Island - 7 in 1983.
Source: Department of Fisheries and Oceans, Annual Statistical Review.

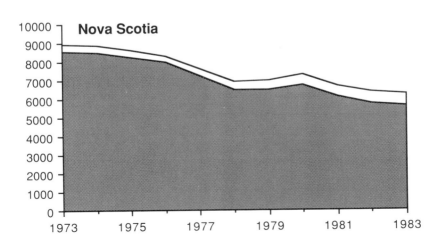

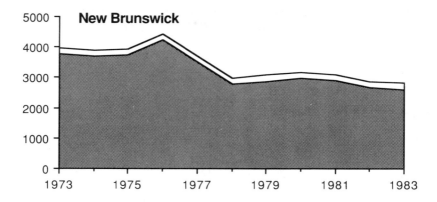

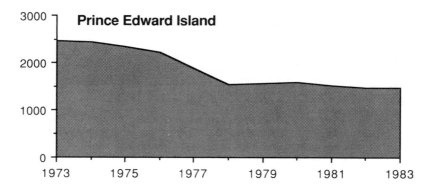

Government and the Fishery

The role of governments in the fishery is no less complex than the industry itself. They manage the resource, administer assistance programs, negotiate quotas and sales internationally, undertake research, and arbitrate between the various interest groups within the sector. It is often difficult to distinguish one role from another.

The nature of fish stocks dictates that much management be a public responsibility. The resource is regarded as "common property" in nature; the business of catching the fish is essentially removed from the business of managing stocks. This management defies the best efforts at regulation, dealing as it does with a resource which is mobile and varies greatly with time.

Management of the resource is primarily a federal responsibility. The need for improved management emerged as the susceptibility of various stocks to overfishing became evident. Before 1977, management was a matter of difficult international negotiations, based on the concept of maximum sustainable yield. This is the maximum harvest which can be taken in a given period without significantly affecting the natural replenishment rate of the fish. An annual Groundfish Management Plan was introduced in 1977, which consolidated existing inshore and offshore quota systems, and established new ones for species not already covered by quota. Biologists set Total Allowable Catches designed to maintain stocks and promote steady growth.

Despite Canada's 200-mile limit, international sensitivities and interests in the northwest Atlantic fishery remain strong. The difficulties of setting national boundaries over the ocean are particularly complex. Canada has had disputes in recent years with the United States over where the boundary lies on Georges Bank (resolved only by reference to the International Court of Justice); and with France over boundaries around St Pierre and Miquelon.

As well as limiting the amount of stocks which can be taken, there are also regulations on the types of vessels and gear which can be used, on the amount of time spent fishing (by establishing seasons, for example), and on the number of fishermen allowed to take part in a fishery (by issuing licences). All measures are designed to participate in managing pressures on a given stock over a given period. They are rarely popular with the fishermen themselves, as they can involve reduction of income-earning capacity.

The regulatory system is undergoing reform in the 1980s. In particular, there is the concept of property rights in the fishery. Acceptance of this will go some way to bringing a common-property resource within the management interests of individual fishermen. They would become more like farmers, with definite incentives to manage their source of livelihood to provide a stream of income over the years. Enterprise allocations have also been introduced, whereby individual processors or plants receive a given quota for a season. This helps prevent the "rush to the fish" in the early part of a season, with subsequent bottlenecks in plants and expensive inventory control.

Fish Processing

Fish processing is a most important component of manufacturing in Atlantic Canada. It is the single most important activity, in terms of either employment or output, in three of the four provinces. In 1984, there were almost 19,000 jobs in fish plants around the region, and the Task Force reported that some 47,000 jobs depended on fish processing in 1980. The number of registered plants increased from 519 in 1977 to 700 in 1981 (including some in Quebec).

In fish processing, as in other manufacturing enterprises, a few companies account for a large proportion of activity. A survey of 100 firms undertaken by the Task Force revealed that sales of six big integrated companies in 1981 accounted for 80% of the industry total. In 1983, after severe financial difficulties, radical restructuring of the industry reduced the number of big companies to two: Fisheries Products International, based in Newfoundland; and National Sea Products, based in Nova Scotia. Injections of public funds (especially into FPI) and subsequent market strength have allowed an almost total return of these companies to private hands. The industry also has many more smaller plants dotted around the region, mostly in small communities and mostly in private hands. Value of shipments of fish products in 1984 was more than $1.4 billion, with 80% of this coming from Newfoundland and Nova Scotia. More than 80% of all fish products are exported, with the most important destinations being the United States, Europe, and Japan.

Fish processing is almost as complex an industry as the primary industry which supplies it with fish, and this complexity frequently relates closely to the nature of the resource. Seasonality of catches, for example, also means seasonality in plants, working full speed at certain times of year, lying idle at others. This entails difficult quality-control problems, oversupply on markets, and lower profit margins.

There are also linkages to other industries in the form of supplies purchased by fishermen, ranging from boats to nets, special clothing, storage boxes, navigation equipment, rope, and much more. Workshops, big and small, supply these items around the region, and have become valuable sources of local employment in their own right.

The Fishery: Some Special Aspects

Nature of the Resource. The fishery is regarded as a common-property resource, where management of fish stocks is essentially separated from catching fish. In terms of economics, fishermen will catch fish until they have dissipated all the economic rent normally attached to a commodity in demand; in lay terms, everybody's business is nobody's business. There is little incentive for the people who benefit from the resource to husband the resource. Governments have undertaken this role.

Although fishermen and farmers are similar in some respects, the resource which underpins their respective endeavours sets them apart. Farmers own rights in land, and can erect fences to define the legal margins of their property. Fishermen cannot erect fences to contain fish (although an emerging aquaculture industry is currently making this more and more of a reality). They must go to where the fish are, or wait for the fish to come to them according to their own biological seasons.

The seasonality of a fisherman's annual work, therefore, is dictated by the resource. Stocks vary according to breeding and migration cycles, which are often imperfectly understood. The sea imposes physical restrictions on when fishermen can work safely. Lack of scientific knowledge hampers management. Incorrect judgements which understate the size of a stock deny fishermen income; those which overstate the stock threaten fishermen's livelihood.

The fishery is a fluctuating industry depending on fish movement, breeding success, and subsequent survival rates. The seasonality spills over into associated industries and markets. Processing plants are built to take peak flows of fish even though this flow may occur for less than a full year. This increases unit overhead costs and plant employment.

Seasonality of a single species can be offset by pursuing other species at different times of year. Lobstermen in many areas, for example, turn with ease to gill-netting for herring and mackerel, or drag for scallops when lobster seasons are closed. Many other fishermen rotate their year between different jobs. To a degree, this traditional aspect of the Atlantic fishery has been reduced by allowing fishermen to qualify for unemployment benefits despite their self-employed status. This has been questioned on the grounds that it may deter the movement of marginal fishermen to other occupations, and perpetuate lower incomes in certain parts of the fishery by artificially inflating the number of fishermen involved in that fishery. It may also perpetuate the role of the sector as a "residual" source of employment, attracting labour in times of recession only to lose it when prosperity returns. It is a fact, however, that local job opportunities for unemployed fishermen are sometimes few and far between, and unemployment benefits offer one alternative source of income when seasons are closed.

A Business or a Social Welfare System? This last point leads directly into the role of the fishery in Atlantic Canada, particularly the small-boat fishery. It has frequently been characterised as being too bound in tradition to be run as an efficient business, although the success of modern offshore fleets should dispel this image. In many cases, the radical rationalisation of the primary fishery would involve profound disruption in many small communities where fishing is the only industry. Few

Fishery

59

politicians contemplate this as a serious option, and most past policy efforts have offered incentives to fishermen to give up licences voluntarily.

Establishment of some kind of property rights in the fishery may begin the process of changing the nature of the resource itself, pushing it away from common property to private equity. Self-interest on the part of participants is seen as an essential step in promoting a more businesslike approach in many cases. Management techniques such as enterprise allocations help prevent the harvesting of large amounts of fish, which must also be processed rapidly or stored, but only released onto markets at a pace which will not depress prices.

Concerns over quality have seen great arguments over adding advanced factory freezer trawlers to the Canadian offshore fleet. These allow processing of fish at sea soon after they have been caught, avoiding delays as boats complete their catches and face a lengthy trip back to home ports to unload at the fish plant. Factory ships mean jobs would be transferred from land to sea, rarely a popular alternative in the communities concerned. Many of the foreign fleets that fish off the East Coast, however, are based on factory ships. Quality of end product has improved in recent years as freezer trawlers (not factory ships) have installed container-based storage systems, as dockside loading and unloading techniques have improved, and as prices have responded to better fish on markets.

Summary

The Task Force on Atlantic Fisheries reflected on the region's marine heritage:

> If the fishery attracted the first settlers to much of Canada's east coast, it has become a bittersweet resource base for their descendants, a resource whose always-bright potential remains just that— potential. There have been good years, to be sure, but they have been part of a cyclical boom and bust pattern that has not captured the potential of the resource with any semblance of stability. . .
> The fishery today does not provide a good living for many of the people who participate in it.[2]

The inability to capitalise on a resource of almost proverbial richness has been a continuing source of frustration. Admittedly, the industry is complex but even declaration of a 200-mile zone has failed to live up to its promise and has not prevented near-collapse of big companies in the early 1980s.

The later 1980s have seen a dramatic resurgence in the fishery based on strong markets in the United States and elsewhere. This is because of changing tastes and eating habits; fish is healthy, low-fat protein. A deterioration in the value of the Canadian dollar in terms of American funds has also helped, as has the industry's constant search for better quality. The industry remains an indispensable part of the larger Atlantic economy, and is rapidly changing. Even the traditional, independent fisherman tends to buy more advanced equipment to help his enterprise. The big integrated companies are expanding market networks and improving their own operations. The Atlantic fishery, quite slowly, may begin to live up to its potential.

Footnotes

1. The Task Force on Atlantic Fisheries is the most recent comprehensive examination of the sector, and reported in 1982. This report is a basic reference for this chapter, and the Task Force will be referred to several times in the pages which follow.

2. Task Force on Atlantic Fisheries, *Navigating Troubled Waters: A New Policy for the Atlantic Fisheries*. (Report of the Task Force, Ottawa, 1982.) p. 6.

Further Reading

Copes, P., "Fisheries Management on Canada's Atlantic Coast: Economic Factors and Socio-Political Constraints" in *The Canadian Journal of Regional Science*, 6(1), Spring 1983, pp1-32.

Fisheries and Oceans Canada, *Canadian Fisheries Annual Statistical Review*. Ottawa, annual.

Fisheries and Oceans Canada, *Atlantic Fishing Methods*. Communications Branch, Ottawa, 1982.

Le Messurier, S.L., *The Fishery of Newfoundland and Labrador*. Edited by S. Sherk, published by the Extension Service, Memorial University of Newfoundland, 1980.

Munro, G.R., *A Promise of Abundance: Extended Fisheries Jurisdiction and the Newfoundland Economy*. Prepared for the Economic Council of Canada, 1980.

Newfoundland and Labrador, Government of, *Report of the Royal Commission to Inquire into the Inshore Fishery of Newfoundland and Labrador*. Brose Paddock, Chairman, St John's, 1981.

Newfoundland Department of Fisheries, *Setting a Course: A Regional Strategy for Development of the Newfoundland Fishing Industry to 1985*. St John's, 1978, four volumes.

Nova Scotia Department of Fisheries, *Sea, Salt & Sweat: A Story of Nova Scotia and the Vast Atlantic Fisheries*. Halifax, 1977.

Task Force on Atlantic Fisheries, *Navigating Troubled Waters: A New Policy for the Atlantic Fisheries*. Report of the Task Force on Atlantic Fisheries, M.J.L. Kirby, Chairman, Ottawa, 1982.

Warner, W.W., *Distant Water: The Fate of the North Atlantic Fisherman*. An Atlantic Monthly Press Book. Boston and Toronto: Little, Brown and Company, 1977 and 1983.

CHAPTER 5

Forestry: The Multiple Resource

Forest-based enterprise has figured prominently in Atlantic economic history since the eighteenth century. Seemingly unlimited stands of conifers supplied the Royal Navy with timber to maintain and expand its fleet of ships and shore facilities. A prosperous domestic shipbuilding industry in the nineteenth century formed the base of a diverse manufacturing economy in the Maritimes. Pulp and paper mills were built in the twentieth century, and many of them remain the principal source of jobs and incomes for individual communities. Sawmills and planing mills turn out lumber for both domestic and export construction industries.

The Woods: More Than Just Trees

The woods are more than an economic reserve of fibre, however. They also provide energy in the form of fuelwood; they are home to a rich and varied wildlife; they are an irreplaceable recreation and leisure resource; and they are indispensable to many natural processes such as groundwater flow and regulation. Management of a resource with so many divergent uses poses a persistent challenge.

Two broad forest regions are represented in Atlantic Canada.[1] The *boreal forest region* typifies Labrador and much of insular Newfoundland. White and black spruces dominate, with stands of other softwoods like tamarack, balsam fir and jack pine; and hardwoods such as white birch, poplar and aspen. The *Acadian forest region* takes in the Maritimes, with red, white, and black spruces, balsam fir, red and white pine, eastern hemlock, yellow birch and sugar maple.

TABLE 5.1: SUMMARY OF LAND AREA UNDER FORESTS, ATLANTIC PROVINCES

	Total Forested Area		Non-Reserved Forest Land (1)		Total Provincial Land Area (2)
	(3)	(4)	(3)	(4)	(3)
Newfoundland and Labrador	338	91.3	335	90.5	370
Prince Edward Island	3	50.0	—	—	6
Nova Scotia	41	77.4	40	75.5	53
New Brunswick	66	91.7	65	90.3	72
Atlantic Canada	448	89.4	440	87.8	501

Notes 1) "Reserved" land is, by law, not available for cutting trees for commercial use. It includes parks and wildlife preserves.
2) Excluding inland water.
3) In millions of hectares.
4) As percentage of total provincial land area.

Source: Statistics Canada Catalogue 25-202.

TABLE 5.2: INVENTORIED PRODUCTIVE AND ECONOMICALLY ACCESSIBLE FOREST AREA, ATLANTIC PROVINCES

	Area	As Percent of Total Forested Area
	– million hectares –	– per cent –
Newfoundland and Labrador	54	16.0
Nova Scotia	38	92.7
New Brunswick	61	92.4
Atlantic Canada	153	34.1

Note: Excluding Prince Edward Island

Source: Statistics Canada Catalogue 25-202

The Canada Land Inventory has devised seven classes to describe a given land area's capability for supporting commercial forestry. Class 1 has no significant limitations, class 7 is essentially unproductive. Although there are pockets of classes 1 to 3 in Atlantic Canada, they are scattered and small. Most Maritime land is in capability classes 4 and 5, with 6 and 7 more common on the island of Newfoundland; Labrador is not covered by the Canada Land Inventory, but probably tends towards lower classes.[2]

Commercial forestry varies in importance from province to province. Prince Edward Island's woods have been exploited to the point where very little of commercial value remains. There is limited cutting of pulpwood for Maritime mills, and some sawmilling. Nova Scotia has a well-developed pulp and paper sector, and several large sawmills among many smaller ones. New Brunswick, with pulp and paper mills and an important lumbering industry, relies to a proportionally greater extent on forestry to drive its economy. Newfoundland has the region's biggest production of newsprint from three mills, but only a small-scale sawmilling industry.

The Resource Base and Primary Production

Almost 90% of Atlantic Canada is covered by trees (Table 5.1). Both Newfoundland and New Brunswick have about 91% of their respective areas under trees, Nova Scotia has about 77% and Prince Edward Island about 50%. Not all of this is available. About 2% is reserved in parks and other recreational or wildlife preservation areas.

Actual *volumes* rather than *areas* of wood are biggest in New Brunswick, both for softwood and hardwood. This province accounts for an estimated 45% of the region's softwood reserves, and 63% of hardwood reserves. Newfoundland's accessible reserves are next, followed by Nova Scotia, although this province's reserves of hardwood are higher than Newfoundland's. The total volume of wood (particularly softwood) harvested from accessible areas has been declining in recent years; hardwood reserves are still substantial compared to requirements.

Commercial forestry depends not only on adequate volumes of the right species (hardwoods and softwoods are not substitutes in many industrial uses, and require different milling processes) but also on their accessibility (Table 5.2). Much of Newfoundland's reserve of woodland is in Labrador, remote from established mills. Accessibility of reserves improves greatly in the Maritimes, with smaller land areas and better-developed road networks.

FIGURE 5.1: OWNERSHIP OF FORESTED LAND, ATLANTIC PROVINCES

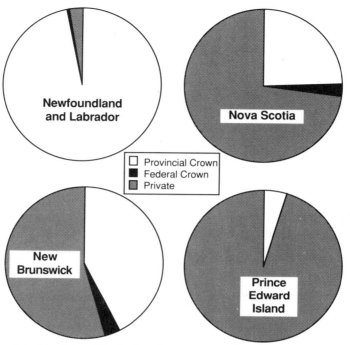

Note: Prince Edward Island estimate based on the 1973 National Inventory Survey.
Source: Canadian Forestry Service (Environment Canada); Statistics Canada 13-202.

FIGURE 5.2: ROUNDWOOD PRODUCTION IN THE ATLANTIC PROVINCES, 1960 AND 1970–1984

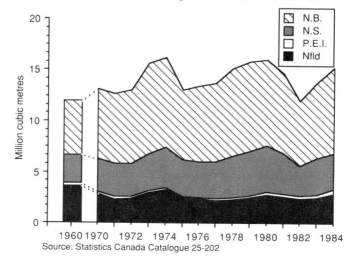

Source: Statistics Canada Catalogue 25-202

Ownership of woodland also affects its accessibility (Figure 5.1). Trees on small, privately-held woodlots are more difficult to cut efficiently, and wide-scale management programs are more difficult to coordinate. In Prince Edward Island, about 5% of the woodland is owned by the Province, while about 94% is privately owned, mostly in 16,000 small woodlots. In contrast, in Newfoundland, where almost 97% of the woodland is provincial Crown land, less than 3% is in private hands. There is a higher incidence of large private woods in Nova Scotia and especially in New Brunswick, but even in these two provinces small woodlots are important (50% in Nova Scotia, 33% in New Brunswick).

About 33% of wood going to mills in Nova Scotia in 1980 was from small private woodlots, smaller than the 37% from large private holdings but larger than the 30% from Crown land. Almost 50% of New Brunswick's wood supplies in 1980 was from Crown land, with the balance split roughly equally between small and large private holdings. Log production in the other provinces corresponds to ownership patterns closely.

Roundwood production is highest in New Brunswick, followed by Nova Scotia, Newfoundland and Prince Edward Island (Figure 5.2). Total volumes cut in the region increased by 34% between 1960 and 1980, with most of the increase occurring in the 1970s, predominantly in New Brunswick and Nova Scotia. Recessions in the mid-1970s and early 1980s demonstrate the vulnerability of forest products to business cycles. In general, reduced demand for lower-value products (especially lumber and pulp) affects many mills in Atlantic Canada. Rapid decline, however, is usually followed by equally rapid recovery.

Most wood cut in New Brunswick is for industrial use, with a small fraction (4% or 5%) for domestic fuel. Industrial use is split roughly 50:50 between sawmills and pulp mills. However, integration of big sawmills with commonly owned pulp mills means that about 60% of wood going to sawmills actually ends up in pulp mills as chips; final use, therefore, is about 65:35 in favour of pulp production. Some 90% of Nova Scotia's cut is for industrial use, with the balance for firewood. Industrial use is 75:25 in favour of pulp mills, once again allowing for shipments of chips from integrated sawmills.

A larger proportion of Newfoundland's logs goes to pulp mills, about 87%, with the remainder split between small sawmills and firewood. Prince Edward Island's limited production of roundwood sees a substantial 30% being used as firewood, with sawlog production in some years going as high as 50% or 60% of total cut.

Forest-based Manufacturing

Industrial use of logs is mainly in sawmills to produce lumber, veneer and the like, and in the pulp and paper industry. In 1984, sawmills accounted for about 4% or 5% of all manufacturing employment in Atlantic Canada (about 3,800 jobs), and 7% or 8% of manufacturing shipments; these numbers probably exclude production from many seasonal mills dotted around the region, which escape official enumeration. Lumber production has remained relatively constant since the 1970s, although New Brunswick has taken up a bigger share of the regional total; employment in mills in New Brunswick has not increased in line, indicating the presence of bigger, automated sawmills usually integrated with pulp and paper mills.

New Brunswick's lumber output depends significantly on export markets in New England, in turn dictated by construction activity. The other three provinces produce mainly for local markets, although Nova Scotia also has some exports. Extremely high interest rates in the early 1980s meant severe decline in construction activity, which cut deeply into mill production. Subsequent lower interest rates led to rapid recovery for those sawmills able to survive the recession of 1981 and 1982.

There are nineteen big pulp and paper mills in Atlantic Canada, and five or six smaller mills producing such things as hardboard, moulded pulp products (egg cartons and the like), and packaging products such as cardboard boxes. Some big mills produce only pulp to a certain grade, and are integrated either with other mills producing paper products in the region, or other commonly-owned mills in other countries. Other mills manufacture mainly newsprint, and one of the newest (in New Brunswick) manufactures higher quality coated or fine paper. These mills employ at least 10,000 workers directly, while many more jobs in the woods and in related industries such as chemicals and trucking depend indirectly on their operation.

Pulp and paper production is one of the most competitive industries in the world. Canada has established itself as the single biggest source of such products, and is adjacent to the world's biggest market; in 1986, 86% of Canadian printing paper exports (mainly newsprint), worth $6.3 billion ($925 from Atlantic Canada), and almost 50% of Canadian pulp exports went to American markets.

Canadian exports have increased as worldwide production capacity has expanded, both in industrialised and less industrialised economies. American domestic production of pulp has doubled since 1960, and its production of newsprint has gone up by 75%. Latin America produces six times as much pulp as it did in 1960, and three times as much newsprint. All these new competitors are export-oriented. Many have either large untouched reserves of forests, or climates where trees grow more quickly than in Canada. Some producers, such as the Scandinavians, have maintained an intense competitive edge by the use of advanced technology. Many Canadian mills, including most of those in Atlantic Canada, have met competition by modernising. It takes a long time for a tree to grow in our northern climate, but the higher quality of the fibre, resulting in higher quality pulp, gives Canada a compensating advantage. Some mills have diversified into higher-value products, such as coated or writing papers.

Because pulp and paper production is energy-intensive, many mills are vulnerable to rising energy costs. Some older mills in Atlantic Canada have associated hydro plants, erected at the same time as the mill and owned and operated by the same owners. Most mills, however, must buy energy; a final aspect of modernisation has been to become much more energy-efficient, or to explore alternative sources of energy such as wood-waste boilers.

Aspects of Forest Management

The Annual Allowable Cut and Fibre Demand. Development of forest-related industries depends on supplies of trees. Forests are regarded as renewable resources because, left to their own devices, they will eventually regenerate and grow back. Annual allowable cuts (AACs) are set by provincial governments (which have main responsibility for managing forest resources) to ensure that demand for fibre does not outstrip supply. AACs are set to reflect annual rate of tree growth, losses to fire and insects, share of the crop which is marketable, and so on.

This has not prevented a rather serious situation developing in Atlantic Canada, where lack of forest management in the past will probably result in medium-term shortages of supplies for mills. The shortfall in Newfoundland could reach as high as 50% of requirements by 2020 in the absence of urgently needed forest development. In Nova Scotia, manufacturers need 3.3 million cubic metres of softwood annually; in the absence of substantial silviculture, the AAC is only 2.4 million cubic metres. There is a shortfall in New Brunswick amounting to 1.4 million cubic metres out of total demand of 6.9 million cubic metres. (All estimates come from provincial commissions or agencies.) Two interrelated problems are partially responsible for this shortage: insect infestation, and imbalanced age structures in commercial stands.

Insect Infestation. Atlantic forests have been, or are being, threatened by a variety of insect pests, such as hemlock looper, bark beetles, forest tent caterpillars, and spruce budworm. The last of these has received most attention in recent decades. The latest outbreak reached New Brunswick in the early 1950s, and reached Newfoundland in 1970 by way of both Nova Scotia and Prince Edward Island. In New Brunswick, an aerial spray program to combat the infestation has been in operation since 1953 but this has not prevented spread of the pest. Trees can survive the loss of new foliage to the budworm several years in a row, but eventually they die. From this point their commercial utility lasts only four or five years, so they must be harvested within that period.

The extent of infestation exceeds attempts to harvest. In Newfoundland in 1980, budworm had severely affected or killed 40 million cubic metres of softwood in spite of a spray program. In Cape Breton alone at the end of 1982, many million hectares of spruce and fir had been lost to the budworm.

Effects of budworm over large areas of softwood can be cumulative. Stands of dead trees are more prone to fire, and provide conditions for development of other pests. Even with light infestation, the seed-bearing capacity of trees is severely impaired. This, in turn, inhibits natural replacement with commercially desirable species. Wildlife habitat and recreational opportunities are affected. Salvage operations which harvest inferior qualities of wood (where deterioration of fibres is well established) affect quality of pulp, paper or lumber. The rate of salvage is limited by mill capacities.

In earlier times an insect outbreak may have been regarded as beneficial when it destroyed decadent stands of trees and cleared space for establishment of new ones; this is not the modern economic view. The problem of controlling pests is compounded by public debate over the methods used. Aerial broadcast of chemicals in New Brunswick and Newfoundland has met a growing and organised resistance from concerned citizens. Biological means may be safer to humans and wildlife, but their effectiveness has been more limited than chemicals, and they tend to be much more expensive. Natural controls are time-consuming and unpredictable.

Ideally, some combination of control methods would restore forests to health if they were part of an integrated, long-term management plan. Both industry and governments have resisted this so far on grounds of cost and time. A characteristic of forest economics is that economic and financial returns on growing trees take much longer than for other investments, especially with a climate such as Canada's. This colours many decisions concerning longer-term forest management, although there

TABLE 5.3: SPECIES GROUP AND MATURITY CLASS ON PROVINCIAL CROWN FOREST LAND, ATLANTIC PROVINCES, 1981

	Newfoundland and Labrador	Nova Scotia	New Brunswick
	– percent of economically accessible volume –		
Softwood:			
Immature	7.9	37.5	12.5
Mature	92.1	56.2	84.3
Uneven Aged	–	6.3	3.1
Hardwood:			
Immature	10.8	35.7	10.5
Mature	89.2	64.3	82.9
Uneven Aged	–	–	6.5

Note: Excluding Prince Edward Island

Source: Statistics Canada Catalogue 25-202

have been notable exceptions where extensive reforestation has occurred on large, privately held lands.

Uneven Age Structures. A commercial forest ideally has reserves of trees of many ages growing at once. There will be a reserve of mature trees being harvested while other stands are in various stages of reaching maturity. This situation rarely occurs in Atlantic Canada, because insect infestation and forest fires have destroyed large areas of trees within a short period.

Estimates of the amount of trees in various maturity classes are in Table 5.3. About 90% of both softwoods and hardwoods in Newfoundland are classified as mature, and 83% in New Brunswick. In Nova Scotia, only about 33% of trees fall into the important age classes that form the backbone of future supply.

Increasing Fibre Supply. Both industry and governments have begun to realise the problems of shortages of wood. Development programs have been written (usually federal-provincial initiatives) which include research and planting programs. Alternative sources of supply are being investigated, such as more output from small woodlots, increased use of hardwood fibre, or more complete utilisation of existing stocks of softwoods.

Management difficulties in one alternative source of supply, small wood-lots, are more complex. The actual area of trees to be managed and cut is smaller, and overhead costs increase accordingly. As not all owners wish their woodlots to be logged, the resource is more dispersed and economies of scale more difficult to achieve. Access for equipment may be restricted.

To a degree, these difficulties can be avoided by owners themselves doing the cutting, and then selling the wood through cooperatives or other group organisations. Nova Scotia and New Brunswick have developed considerable experience in this respect. Cooperation, especially, allows small woodlot owners a modicum of bargaining strength in setting prices when faced with just a few big buyers.

Summary

Trees are regarded as one of Atlantic Canada's most important resources. This consideration extends beyond their commercial value, to recreation, wildlife, environmental integrity, and natural processes. They also provide many people with alternative energy supplies in the form of firewood. Commercial considerations tend to dominate, however, as important sawmilling and pulp and paper industries testify. These industries have been successful in intensively competitive global markets.

The challenge facing forest industries does not end with maintaining market shares; it also involves a secure supply of wood from the region's woods to maintain output. Many decades of inadequate management practices have resulted in a degree of neglect in the Atlantic forest that almost certainly will result in shortages into the early part of the twenty-first century.

Shortages can be averted to a degree by increasing usage of other forms of fibre, or bringing untapped supplies into play. These should not be substitutes for an integrated, long-term set of programs for reforestation and silviculture. Only by replacing cut or lost trees with healthy, disease- and insect-resistant strains can the sector face the future with any assurance.

Footnotes:

1. These forest regions were defined by J.S. Rowe, *Forest Regions of Canada*, Bulletin 123, Forestry Branch, Department of Northern Affairs and National Resources, Ottawa, 1959. Further detail has been added in O.L. Loucks, *A Forest Classification for the Maritime Provinces*, reprinted from the Proceedings of the Nova Scotia Institute of Science, Vol. 25, Part 2, 1959-60.

2. More discussion on the Canada Land Inventory capability classes for forestry are in W. Simpson-Lewis *et al., Canada's Special Resource Lands: A National Perspective of Selected Land Uses,* Lands Directorate, Environment Canada, Map Folio No. 4, Ottawa, 1979.

Further Reading

Bonnor, G.M., *Canada's Forest Inventory 1981.* Forestry Statistics and Systems Branch, Canadian Forestry Service, Environment Canada, Ottawa, 1982.

Canadian Pulp and Paper Association, *Reference Tables,* Montreal, annual.

New Brunswick Department of Natural Resources, *New Brunswick Forestry Development Strategy for the Eighties.* Fredericton, 1982. Nova Scotia Department of Lands and Forests, Submission to the Royal Commission on Forestry. Halifax, 1983.

Nova Scotia Department of Lands and Forests, *Submission to the Royal Commission on Forestry.* Halifax, 1983.

Royal Commission on Forest Protection and Management, *Report.* C.F. Poole, Chairman, St John's, 1981, two volumes.

The Economist, "Papermakers Learn Origami." Industry Brief, February 7, 1987, pp70-71.

CHAPTER 6

Mining: Earthly Riches

Atlantic Canada's land provides more than a medium in which to grow crops or trees; it also contains a rich diversity of minerals. These are closely linked to the geological history of the region. The very old rocks of the Shield in Labrador contain immense reserves of high quality iron ore. The contorted rocks of northern New Brunswick have valuable mineralised zones rich in ores of gold, silver, zinc, lead, and copper. Younger sedimentary basins in Nova Scotia and New Brunswick have extensive coal deposits. Gypsum, salt and potash are quarried or mined in Newfoundland, Nova Scotia and New Brunswick. Sand, stone and gravel pits provide construction materials throughout the region; this is the only mineral enterprise in Prince Edward Island. Clays of various types are quarried in Newfoundland, Nova Scotia, and New Brunswick with important local linkages to brick and cement manufacture.

Mineral extraction accounts for appreciable shares of goods-producing gross domestic product in Newfoundland (12%) and to a lesser extent Nova Scotia and New Brunswick. Many small and often isolated communities depend mainly on mining for their existence, including Labrador City (iron ore); Pugwash, Nova Scotia (salt); and Chipman-Minto, New Brunswick (coal).

The economics of mineral extraction involve a number of considerations: location; quantity and quality of deposit; extractive and refining technology; markets and prices; substitute materials; and many others.

TABLE 6.1: OUTPUT OF SELECTED MINERALS IN ATLANTIC PROVINCES, 1965, 1976, AND 1985

	1965	1976	1985
	– percent of total value of provincial mineral output –		
Newfoundland and Labrador:			
Iron ore	78.0	87.0	90.1
Copper	5.5	—	—
Lead	3.4	0.6	—
Zinc	5.4	5.1	4.1
Asbestos	4.4	4.5	2.2
Nova Scotia:			
Coal	73.1	62.3	51.5
Gypsum	13.9	15.9	15.9
Salt	7.4	15.0	n/a
New Brunswick:			
Zinc	51.5	55.0	53.2
Silver	4.7	8.4	9.5
Lead	18.6	25.0	7.7
Potash	—	—	5.7
Coal	11.9	3.0	5.4
Copper	10.4	7.0	2.4
Peat	1.9	2.3	2.4

Sources: Statistics Canada Catalogue 26-202; New Brunswick Department of Natural Resources and Energy.

Types of Minerals in Atlantic Canada

Iron ore has dominated mining in Newfoundland and Labrador since deposits in Labrador were first developed in the early 1960s (Table 6.1). Other types of minerals produced include asbestos, gypsum, and fluorspar. Base metals were mined until the mid-1980s, when the deposits were exhausted. Silica is extracted on the Avalon Peninsula and goes to a reduction plant nearby to produce phosphorus. Rich deposits of gold-bearing ores near Port aux Basques are being developed in the late 1980s.

Coal, salt, gypsum, and tin are the principal minerals produced in Nova Scotia. There are coal fields in northern Nova Scotia (in Cumberland and Pictou counties) and in eastern Cape Breton Island. The Cape Breton mines have a current output of about 2 million tonnes a year, most of which is burnt in electricity plants. Cape Breton's mines were due to be closed in the late 1960s, and a federal agency, the Cape Breton Development Corporation, was established to manage the closure. However, big increases in the price of oil in the mid- and late 1970s, and overdependence for electricity generation on imported oil, caused a reversal of the decision. New mines have been developed as coal has substantially replaced oil in power stations.

Gypsum comes mainly from the Windsor area, with some from southern Cape Breton. Most gypsum is manufactured into wallboard, and sales depend closely on ups and downs in the North American construction industry. Salt is extracted in Pugwash and near Amherst, and is used mainly for de-icing roads in winter. The province's tin mine in Yarmouth County has been operating only since 1985. It is an important new development in an area known for its mineral potential, but with little real development as yet. New gold mines are being developed in central Nova Scotia in the late 1980s.

Principal mineral output in New Brunswick is of base metals, precious metals, and potash. In the north of the province is the world's biggest zinc mine, with associated production of lead, copper, and silver. This same area has established reserves of gold-bearing ores. Also in northern New Brunswick is a lead smelter, Atlantic Canada's main mineral refining capacity. Peat is processed in the northeastern part of the province, and coal in the central part. Potash mines in the southern part started operations in 1984; they have salt as a byproduct. In the recent past, tungsten and molybdenum have been mined in Charlotte County, and Canada's only operational antimony mine is near Fredericton.

Total value of mineral production in Atlantic Canada has increased greatly since 1961 (Figure 6.1 and Table 6.2). A value of $1.8 billion in 1985 is more than 10 times higher than in 1961 in nominal terms, and represents an annual average rate of change of 10.3%. Some 90% of Newfoundland's value is for iron ore, and output from Labrador's mines strongly influences total value of regional mineral output; dips in 1978 and the early 1980s (see Figure 6.1) reflect a strike in the iron mines and economic recession respectively. The vulnerability of low-value products, such as iron ore, to business cycles was sharply demonstrated in 1982, when Newfoundland's mineral production dipped by 37% from 1981.

Minerals are exported either as raw materials (mainly iron, base metal or precious metal ores or concentrates, coal, asbestos or gypsum) or in manufactured form such as lead, phosphorus and fertiliser. The value of raw material export in 1986 was about $1 billion, mostly iron and zinc ores, gypsum, coal, and asbestos. Most of New Brunswick's important zinc ore production is destined initially for refining in Quebec. Patterns of mineral export are influenced by mine ownership; substantial interests

FIGURE 6.1: VALUE OF MINERAL PRODUCTION, ATLANTIC PROVINCES, 1961–1984

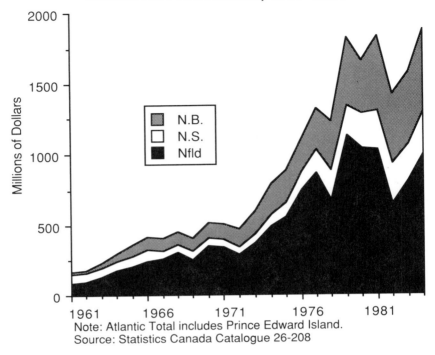

Note: Atlantic Total includes Prince Edward Island.
Source: Statistics Canada Catalogue 26-208

TABLE 6.2: TOTAL VALUE OF MINERAL OUTPUT [1], ATLANTIC PROVINCES [2] AND CANADA 1961, 1966, 1971, 1976 AND 1980–1985

	Newfoundland and Labrador	Nova Scotia	New Brunswick	Atlantic Canada	Canada
	– $ million –				
1961	91.6	61.7	18.8	172.2	2,582.3
1966	238.3	68.3	79.2	385.8	3,972.8
1971	343.4	60.1	107.2	476.1	5,962.7
1976	745.0	125.1	236.0	1,057.1	15,442.7
1980	1,035.7	246.7	372.5	1,654.9	31,841.7
1981	1,030.3	268.3	531.0	1,830.1	32,420.2
1982	646.8	281.2	493.0	1,421.0	33,837.0
1983	807.0	260.2	506.0	1,573.2	38,539.0
1984	979.2	303.8	613.0	1,896.0	43,788.8
1985	927.1	327.8	550.3	1,805.2	44,875.3

Notes 1) Excluding oil and gas   Source: Statistics Canada Catalogue 26-202
2) Excluding Prince Edward Island

TABLE 6.3: MINING EMPLOYMENT (INCLUDING MILLING) ATLANTIC PROVINCES 1961, 1971, 1981, AND 1986

	Newfoundland and Labrador	Nova Scotia	New Brunswick	Atlantic Canada
1961	3,300	8,058	1,342	12,100
1971	5,358	5,400	2,417	13,175
1981	5,600	4,700	3,100	14,400
1986	2,500	6,000	4,400	12,900

Sources: Statistics Canada Catalogue 72-516 (1961, 1971, and 1981); Provincial government estimates (1986).

in Labrador iron mines are held by American steel firms, which also take large proportions of output.

Mining employment, which has also increased over the years, has changed in nature since 1981 (Table 6.3). Recession in 1982 dealt a severe blow to iron mines in Labrador, and total provincial mine employment has declined by almost 3,000 since then. Modest gains are foreseen in Newfoundland as new or refurbished mines begin operating. Nova Scotia has new coal, tin, and gold operations, and New Brunswick has had potash developments since 1984, and new gold prospects. The overall employment picture in 1986, therefore, is not too different from 1981 although individual components have changed.

Some Aspects of Mineral Production

Commercial Mineral Deposits. The viability of a mineral deposit, and the decision to develop it, is based on several things: its size and quality; location; prices; costs of mining, milling, and transportation. The weight each exerts varies from mineral to mineral. For metallic minerals, the higher the price, the lower the mineral content required to make extraction profitable. The price of iron is relatively low, so high quality and easily extracted ores such as those in Labrador are required to make mining economic. Molybdenum in concentrations of as little as 0.5% and gold in such minute concentrations as 0.3 ounces per ton of ore may be profitable.

Metallic ores usually contain a variety of metals as elements or compounds in close association. The most abundant of these may be justification for extraction, but the nature of markets often erodes margins. In these circumstances, co-products or byproducts are valuable buffers. For example, zinc is the principal product at Brunswick Mining and Smelting's mine in northern New Brunswick, but co-production of lead, copper, and silver is also important. New Brunswick's gold production in 1984 was valued at $7.6 million, exclusively as a byproduct of other mineral production.

Non-metallic minerals do not usually occur as ores, and associated minerals are usually undesirable. Criteria for extraction of these materials are different. Unit prices are usually low, so the main criteria are large uniform deposits of the desired mineral, acceptable quality, ease of extraction, and little associated waste. Atlantic examples are coal, gypsum, asbestos, sand and gravel, limestone, and peat. Many occur abundantly around the world, so final use should be within easy shipping distance of deposit; low value, high bulk commodities cannot bear high transportation costs.

Markets and Prices. Although most of the mineral production in Canada (especially metals) is controlled by a few interests, this pattern stops at the country's frontiers. Global markets in mineral products are highly competitive, mainly because most minerals occur abundantly around the globe.

Markets for raw or semi-raw commodities are fickle. Consumer decisions not to buy that new car or washing machine yet, and to delay building a home for a year or two affect demand for iron ore, zinc, gypsum and many other minerals. Non-cyclical developments also strongly affect demand for minerals; for example, advances in fibre optics in telecommunications equipment reduce demand for copper wiring; other development of substitute materials, such as plastics or ceramics, will further threaten demand for minerals.

Prices of minerals respond quickly to all these, and many more, influences. Mines may be closed, and jobs lost. Sometimes this coincides more or less with exhaustion of known workable or economic deposits, so the closure is permanent. Sometimes, the closure is temporary, awaiting better prices and stronger markets. The longer a mine stays closed, however, the more difficult it is to re-open; flooding in shafts may occur, equipment deteriorate, and skilled workers drift away to other jobs.

There are other influences on mineral prices. Precious metals such as gold and silver are regarded as stores of value. During periods of high inflation there will be increased demand for these metals, not as industrial inputs, but as hedges against money losing its value. Political instability can spur inflation, as turmoil in Iran in the late 1970s (coupled with that country's position as an important oil supplier) amply demonstrated; the price of an ounce of gold soared to more than $800 (U.S.). Increases in gold prices renew interest in old gold-bearing districts. Atlantic Canada has benefited from such price increases in the late 1980s.

Some minerals are also regarded as "strategic", important as inputs in industries in turn regarded as key to national security. This is particularly so when the only known supplies of these minerals are in areas vulnerable to armed conflict or undesirable political influence. Global developments can prompt a country to build up its stockpiles of key minerals (Canada regards chromium and manganese as strategically vital) and also spur further exploration on promising areas.

Technology and Labour Costs. The structure of mining industries around the world, many in competition with Canada, varies widely, as does quality of ore mined. Costs of production are most important in maintaining competitive advantage. Typically, wage levels in the Canadian industry are amongst the highest in the world. To compete with Third World producers, therefore, productivity in Canadian mines must also be high. Mining technology has received special attention in the Canadian context to address productivity. Advanced techniques of mining have meant, for example, that Canadian copper producers can extract and refine metal from ores with an average concentration of 0.6%; this competes successfully with ores in Zaire with concentrations of more than 4%.

Labour costs in mining will have special significance in Atlantic Canada if offshore oil and gas fields are developed. Energy and mining industries tend to demand, and compete for, similar skills. The experience of western Canada during the oil and gas boom of the 1970s shows average weekly wages in mineral fuel industries pulled wages in metal mining upwards at a rate substantially faster than the average for all industries. If Atlantic mines are to keep labour, they will have to raise wages; in some cases, this would make mines only marginally profitable. Wages in mining are already amongst the highest in any industry, more than $700 per week in 1986 compared to an all-industry average of $430. A heavier emphasis on mining in Newfoundland means that this province's all-industry average weekly wage is the highest in Atlantic Canada, with New Brunswick second for similar reasons.

Linkages to Other Sectors. Metallic ores go through several stages before they are ready to be incorporated into consumer or capital goods. Extraction is normally followed by beneficiation of the ore, then comminution, concentration, and refining. The refined metal is then ready for further manufacture into recognisable end products.

Little beyond concentration of Atlantic mineral ores actually occurs in the region, and some (such as iron ore) are only beneficiated to reduce bulk for shipping. Lead is smelted and refined in northern New Brunswick (with associated production of sulphuric acid and fertiliser), and steel rails are manufactured at Sydney, Nova Scotia. There are a number of other metallurgical works in northern Nova Scotia and elsewhere in the region, and many smaller machine shops doing largely custom work for local markets. Clay and limestone are manufactured into construction materials such as bricks or concrete. Most other minerals (metallic and non-metallic) are shipped in raw or semi-processed form, and much of the value added to these resources by subsequent manufacture occurs elsewhere.

Minerals and Frontier Development. Mineral extraction offers a way to develop areas and regions otherwise considered remote. This has occurred in Labrador (where a 560-km railway brings iron ore to the Gulf of St Lawrence, and complete new towns have been built) and in the interior of northern New Brunswick and western Nova Scotia.

The degree of remoteness dictates the extent of further economic activity. Interior Labrador remains quite inaccessible, although construction of the Trans-Labrador highway with mining towns at one end, and the Atlantic Ocean at the other, may reduce this further. Remoteness, however, is still a barrier to development of other industries such as tourism. In the Maritimes the mere construction of a road to a mining site can open an area to further developments such as tourism and forestry. The establishment of the first mine in an area often provides a focus for further mineral exploration; areas rich in minerals usually offer more than one opportunity for development, a fact well demonstrated in northern New Brunswick.

Exploration for minerals usually begins with geological surveys. Maps can only indicate broad areas of potential, which is a far cry from precise identification and delineation of deposits. For a long time, exploration was the domain of the individual prospector, whose image now forms a part of the Canadian identity. Then so-called junior companies became substantial forces in exploration and development of deposits, to be followed by integration into the operations of the biggest companies. Such companies have increased their stakes in all stages of exploration and development to minimise risks in an era of increasing competition around the world.

Summary

The intrinsic value of various minerals varies widely; it would take tons of sand, gravel, gypsum, or iron ore to equal the value of an ounce of gold. These values also vary over time; salt was one of the most sought-after and expensive of minerals in the Middle Ages, but is now common. Mining is, therefore, an unusually dynamic industry, responding to demands for its products, and constrained by the non-renewable nature of the basic resources.

Atlantic Canada has generous endowments of many minerals, and in some has built up a world leadership. The dynamic nature of the region's industry is demonstrated by 1980s' development of potash, tin, and gold to compensate for some loss of base metal and iron ore capacity. Further developments may see manufacture of coal into a form of crude petroleum which could be further refined into oil products. New exploration is a constant theme, as is investigation of older or previously worked deposits. Mine development can lead to the opening up of remote areas and the stimulation of new exploration once initial infrastructure is installed. Mining's role in overall economic development is vital in Atlantic Canada.

Further Reading

Energy Mines and Resources Canada, *Canadian Minerals Yearbook*. Mineral Policy Sector, Ottawa, annual.

Energy Mines and Resources Canada, *Principal Mineral Areas of Canada*. Map 900A, 1:7,603,200, Mineral Policy Sector and Geological Survey of Canada, Thirty Fifth Edition, Ottawa, 1985.

Marshall, I.B., *Mining, Land Use, and the Environment 1: A Canadian Overview*. Lands Directorate, Environment Canada, Land Use in Canada Series Number 22, Ottawa, 1982.
Especially chapters 2 and 3.

New Brunswick Department of Natural Resources, *Minerals Strategy Update*. Fredericton, 1982.

Nickel, P.E. *et al.*, *Economic Impacts and Linkages of the Canadian Mining Industry*. National Impact of Mining Series Number 6, Centre for Resource Studies, Queen's University Kingston, 1978.

Nova Scotia Department of Mines and Energy, *Coal in Nova Scotia*. Halifax, 1985.

CHAPTER 7

Energy: Heating Homes, Driving Industry

The more advanced an industrial economy becomes, the more energy it needs. This is not, moreover, a straight-line relationship, but is exponential; the amount of energy required increases at a faster rate than the degree of industrialisation. It has been estimated, for example, that total consumption of energy in primitive gathering societies one million years ago amounted to 5,500 calories per person per day. As society evolved (through hunting, various agricultural and industrial stages, into modern industry) so energy consumption increased rapidly. In the mid-1980s, North Americans and their many industries consume on average some 630,000 calories daily, about 115 times more than their primitive ancestors.[1]

Energy industries, deriving demand for their products from other parts of a modern economy, have therefore become integral parts of the same economic structure. They assume greater importance in a northerly country such as Canada, with its long winters and long distances between markets. Much of the evolution of energy supplies in Atlantic Canada has been in developments in electricity generation and transmission networks. Methods of generation vary, from indigenous coal supplies to imported oil, to hydro power and nuclear reaction.

FIGURE 7.1: INSTALLED GENERATING CAPACITY, ATLANTIC PROVINCES, 1961, 1971, AND 1984

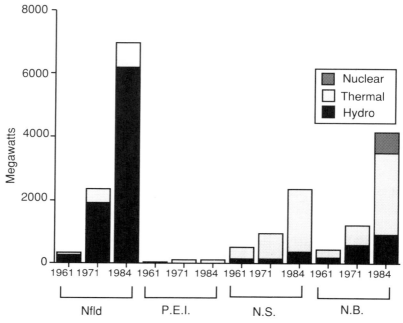

Source: Statistics Canada Catalogue 57-202

Source: Statistics Canada Catalogue 57-202

TABLE 7.1: GENERATING CAPACITY BY PRINCIPAL TYPE, ATLANTIC PROVINCES AND CANADA 1985

	Newfoundland and Labrador	Prince Edward Island	Nova Scotia	New Brunswick	Canada
	– Megawatts –				
Hydro	6,340	—	366	903	56,295
Thermal	756	122	1,849	2,576	30,493
Steam—coal	—	—	875	285	17,186
Steam—oil	505	71	793	1,561	6,043
Int. combustion	81	11	1	5	579
Gas turbine	170	41	180	23	2,362
Nuclear	—	—	—	680	11,159
Total	7,096	122	2,215	3,479 [1]	97,947[2]

Notes 1) Includes 22 MW of "other" types of steam generation.
2) Includes 4,323 MW of gas and "other" types of steam generation.

Source: Energy Mines and Resources Canada, *Electric Power in Canada 1985*. Ottawa, 1986.

Development of Generating Capacity

Electricity is a means of delivering other forms of energy (coal, oil, moving water) more conveniently to markets. Early development of electricity supplies was essentially localised, frequently based on small hydro stations many of which still operate today. Where a bigger demand for power existed (for example, when a pulp mill was built) bigger stations were established; in some cases these were built by the mill owners themselves, who also supplied the entire community with power. As technology allowed expansion of supply grids, fewer and bigger stations were built, supplying markets over much wider areas. Integration of power grids allowed interprovincial exchanges.

The time since the early 1960s has seen electricity develop from localised markets to a commodity traded not only between provinces, but also between nations. Exports especially grew rapidly during the 1970s when the world price of all energy increased sharply; exports to New England from Atlantic Canada were valued at $277 million in 1986. As oil prices went up as well, so established means of generating power were examined. All the provinces had become highly dependent on imported oil for generation. Responses varied: Nova Scotia abruptly switched from a phased decline of Cape Breton's coalfields to a rapid expansion; Newfoundland and New Brunswick undertook big hydro stations, with the latter province also building the region's first nuclear reactor; Prince Edward Island, with no economic alternative means of generating electricity, bought more and more of its supplies from New Brunswick.

Installed generating capacity in the region in 1985 was almost 13,000 MW, or 13.2% of the national total. In 1961, there were only 1,322 MW as installed capacity (Figure 7.1). One project accounts for some 45% of this increase—Churchill Falls in Labrador. This alone has a capacity of 5,225 MW, a figure which tends to skew all considerations of the electricity industry in Atlantic Canada.[2]

The principal means of generation are by moving water, burning coal or oil, and nuclear fission (Table 7.1). This mix has changed over the years, most importantly since the Saint John River was dammed at Mactaquac to produce the region's first major modern hydro station in 1970. About 60% of installed capacity in 1985 is hydro-powered. Mostly, this involves falling water; a variation on this theme began production in 1985 with a pilot tidal power plant at Annapolis Royal, Nova Scotia.

Reliance on water dictates largely where structures must be built, either where natural features provide an existing headpond, or where they can

TABLE 7.2: FUEL USED BY UTILITIES (OTHER THAN HYDRO) TO GENERATE ELECTRICITY, ATLANTIC PROVINCES AND CANADA 1961, 1971, AND 1985

	Coal ('000 t)	Oil (cubic metres)	Uranium (tonnes)
Newfoundland and Labrador:			
1961	—	28,987	—
1971	—	90,097	—
1985	—	459,132	—
Prince Edward Island:			
1961	—	34,935	—
1971	—	100,508	—
1985	64[1]	5,630	—
Nova Scotia:			
1961	555	87,876	—
1971	851	619,187	—
1985	2,153	196,069	—
New Brunswick:			
1961	185	42,182	—
1971	330	692,152	—
1985	486	599,357	120
Canada:			
1961	2,483	396,587	—
1971	18,969	1,956,838	—
1985	38,897	1,413,897	909
Atlantic as % of Canada:			
1961	29.8	48.9	—
1971	6.1	76.8	—
1985	6.9	89.1	13.2

Note 1) Maritime Electric (the electric utility for Prince Edward Island) owns a 10% share in the Dalhousie II power plant in New Brunswick. This coal is purchased by Maritime Electric for burning at this plant; there is no coal-burning capacity in Prince Edward Island.

Sources: Statistics Canada Catalogue 57-202; Energy Mines and Resources Canada, *Electric Power in Canada 1985,* Ottawa 1986.

easily accommodate a dam to create a headpond. Dams are particularly attractive features of hydro developments, as they allow scope for regulating water-flow through turbines to match energy supply better with fluctuations in demand.

All the provinces except Prince Edward Island have big hydro installations. Suitable sites for developments, however, have become more rare and more remote. Most accessible sites have already been used; are already under, or close to, some kind of other use; or are cherished for environmental or recreational reasons. There is still a cluster of sites available in Labrador, however, including expansion of capacity on the Churchill River (both at Churchill Falls and further downstream at Muskrat Falls and Gull Island). There is a series of rivers, as well, which rises in Labrador and flows southwards to the Gulf of St Lawrence through Quebec. These rivers also offer attractive hydro potential amounting to an estimated 8,000 MW.

Hydro developments of the scale built in Canada over the past few decades have been predicated on availability of capital and export markets. The Churchill Falls experience in this respect has not been happy. All output from the site must be transmitted through Quebec to market; the project, indeed, would not have been undertaken if Hydro-Québec had not agreed to buy most of the output, to raise capital, and to build transmission lines. When this agreement was finally made in the late 1960s, energy prices were much lower, and Labrador hydro in the mid 1980s still sells under contract for the equivalent of $1.80 per barrel of oil. All efforts to renegotiate the contract to reflect higher energy prices have failed, and the government of Newfoundland loses an estimated $500 million a year in revenue.

Much Atlantic demand for electricity is still met by thermal generation, mostly steam power using coal or oil. This means of generation is still very important in the Maritime provinces and on the island of Newfoundland. The importance of oil as a feedstock has declined as prices have risen, although it still accounts for 27% of all conventional thermal generation in the region. Some 89% of all oil burnt to generate electricity in Canada in 1985 was in Atlantic stations, with Newfoundland and New Brunswick being especially high consumers (Table 7.2). Newfoundland, indeed, is faced with the dilemma of having to build new oil-burning capacity to supply its internal markets on the island. All suitable hydro sites have been developed, and access to abundant power from Labrador is hampered by current contract arrangements with Quebec, and by the engineering challenge of building transmission lines across the Strait of Belle Isle.

Nova Scotia has greatly expanded its coal-burning capacity, which substantially rescued Cape Breton's coal mines from closure. The province still toys with the idea of tidal generation in the Bay of Fundy, and is examining the operations of its pilot plant closely. Realisation of a big tidal project will require large amounts of capital and resolution of environmental and engineering problems, probably without precedent.

There are other indicators of the expansion of the electrical generating

TABLE 7.3: TRANSMISSION LINE LENGTH, EMPLOYEES, AND NUMBERS OF CUSTOMERS SERVED, ATLANTIC PROVINCES 1961, 1971, 1985

	Newfoundland and Labrador	Prince Edward Island	Nova Scotia	New Brunswick
Transmission line (km):				
1961	n/a	n/a	n/a	n/a
1971	4,363	348	4,692	4,594
1985	5,658	454	4,766	5,873
Employees:				
1961	600	177	1,567	1,244
1971	1,540	194	2,274	1,357
1985	1,908	235	2,417	2,224
Customers:				
1961	70,750	23,541	204,611	156,210
1971	120,443	32,596	252,283	194,892
1985	185,739	47,839	349,944	325,979

Source: Statistics Canada Catalogue 57-202

industry (Table 7.3). The length of transmission line (excluding distribution lines) in the mid-1980s is 20% higher than in 1971. Utilities employed 5,784 people in 1985 compared with 3,588 in 1971. Numbers of customers served within Atlantic Canada have doubled since 1961. All indicate a sophisticated component of the Atlantic economy.

Supply and Disposition of Electricity

The regional electricity industry has gone, in a few years, from supplying essentially localised markets to large-scale interprovincial and international sales (Table 7.4). Movements of power between provinces were limited in 1971 (about 4% of total energy transmitted) although exports were already becoming important (about 9% of total generation). The situation in the mid-1980s sees 56% of total energy generation going to other provinces, and 9% being exported to the United States.

Inter-provincial movements see mostly New Brunswick power going to Prince Edward Island, and Labrador power going to Quebec. International trade involves sales by New Brunswick to utilities in New England. New Brunswick's location allows it to act as a broker in selling electricity, and the total of its sales may not necessarily be of its own generation, but may at any time include some resale of Quebec power.

TABLE 7.4: SUPPLY AND DISPOSITION OF ELECTRICAL ENERGY, ATLANTIC PROVINCES 1971 AND 1985

	Newfoundland and Labrador	Prince Edward Island	Nova Scotia	New Brunswick
	– Gigawatt hours –			
Production:				
1971	5,031	274	4,115	5,680
1985	41,387	2	7,511	11,422
Exports to provinces:				
1971	260	—	145	189
1985	31,837	—	199	927
Exports to U.S.:				
1971	—	—	—	1,335
1985	—	—	—	6,093
Imports:				
1971	—	—	152	462
1985	—	575	350	6,038
Consumption:				
1971	4,771	274	4,122	4,618
1985	9,550	577	7,662	10,440

Note: (Consumption) = (Production) less (Exports to Provinces) less (Exports to U.S.) plus (Imports)

Sources: Statistics Canada Catalogue 57-202; Energy Mines and Resources Canada, *Electric Power in Canada 1985,* Ottawa 1986.

As already mentioned, Prince Edward Island depends almost exclusively on electricity from New Brunswick plants (the province owns a 10% share in a New Brunswick power plant) and its installed capacity has been reduced mostly to meeting periods of peak demand. The Island has extensive experience of experimenting with unconventional methods of generation. These have mostly been small-scale and decentralised, including solar panels, windmills, and low-head hydro. The feasibility of a larger-scale wood-burning generator has also been examined, but the high cost, high bulk nature of wood relative to its heat value make this an unlikely alternative. In any case, Prince Edward Island relies more than the other provinces on wood to heat homes, and it is doubtful whether domestic wood supplies could easily accommodate extra demand to feed a generator without substantial increases in price.

TABLE 7.5: EXAMPLES OF RESIDENTIAL POWER RATES IN SELECTED CITIES IN CANADA, 1971, 1985, AND 1986

	1971	1985	1986	% change 1971–1986
	– dollars for 5000 kWh for lights appliances and heat –			– percent –
St John's	63.27	336.30	314.15	+527.8
Charlottetown	87.66	558.79	536.94	+637.4
Halifax	70.00	292.54	292.54	+417.4
Moncton	70.10	223.68	235.30	+319.1
Montreal	53.20	183.70	188.44	+345.3
Toronto	64.34	238.51	247.69	+370.7
Winnipeg	41.81	155.96	165.35	+373.0
Regina	63.54	224.06	224.06	+352.6
Edmonton	52.00	220.30	234.70	+473.7
Vancouver	60.70	223.81	227.98	+268.7
Yellowknife	n/a	467.00	445.99	n/a

Source: Statistics Canada Catalogue 57-203

Price of Energy

Atlantic Canada has the highest electricity rates nationwide, and has long occupied this unenviable position (Table 7.5; these are residential rates, but commercial and industrial rates are similarly higher than in other parts of Canada.) The gap between rates in the region has widened over the year, with only modest decreases between 1985 and 1986, largely reflecting cheaper oil. These high rates result from four relatively small provinces having at least one utility (there are two major utilities in Newfoundland, and several smaller municipal systems throughout the region). The nature of the market, as well, means extra costs to reach highly dispersed customers; overhead costs increase accordingly. There have been several attempts to set up a regional power grid; the most recent suggestion, from Prince Edward Island, is for marketing at least to be regional in an effort to equalise rates.

Themes in Electricity Generation

Capital versus Operating Costs. Modern electrical plants all require great amounts of money to build, but the relation between capital and operating costs varies between different types of generation. Hydro and nuclear plants need more capital to build, but once built are inexpensive to run, as fuel costs are low. Capital costs can vary substantially during periods of rapidly changing interest rates. Conventional thermal plants are relatively inexpensive to build, but are usually more expensive to run, as operating costs can vary widely as fuel costs change.

There are other factors affecting different kinds of plant. Modern hydro plants are usually remote from markets, which means more capital spending on transmission lines. Nuclear plants require special safeguard mechanisms because of the nature of the feedstock. Increasingly, coal-burning stations must install equipment to clean atmospheric emissions, or investigate means to make the original feedstock cleaner before burning. There is general consensus that the cheapest electrical power comes from nuclear plants. Against this must be set the antipathy with which many people regard nuclear fuel.

Peaking and Pricing of Electrical Power. Because it is very difficult to store, electrical power usually must be consumed as it is produced. This poses complex problems for utilities, because demand for energy varies widely between different times of day and between different seasons of the year. Daily peaks occur early in the day as households and workplaces gear up for the day's activities, and around supper-time. In Canada, seasonal peaks occur both in the depths of winter (when heating costs are higher) and at the height of summer (when cooling costs are higher).

Utilities must build necessary capacity to meet peak demands, or must arrange for reliable purchases from other utilities as a substitute. This means that, for longish periods, capacity to supply exceeds demand. This is a difficult problem for the utilities given the expense of building and operating capacity. Load forecasting has become a highly specialised skill within electrical utilities.

There is also a constant search for methods to increase non-peak use and to decrease peak demand. If this were accomplished, the utility would be able to operate with a lower capacity with savings to consumers as overhead costs come down. As peak demand is often met by using more expensive feedstocks, further savings can be realised. Base loads, for example, may be cheaper hydro or nuclear; peak loads may be gasoline or diesel, which are more expensive but easier to start up.

Methods to even out variations in demand have included time-of-use rates both to increase base demand and reduce peak demand. This is one aspect of a most complex pricing problem facing utilities. Economic efficiency dictates that price of a product be set equal to its marginal cost of the last unit produced. Identifying this cost for electricity is difficult for a variety of reasons: the industry's characteristics of natural monopoly; its public responsibilities and accountability; the industry's cost structure, which tends to favour capital (fixed) costs; and the fact that different types of fuel (which means different operating costs) are used at different times to produce electricity.

Pricing of power, therefore, has evolved along a number of paths in Canada, with rates being set more to fulfil a number of objectives rather than cover marginal costs. These include:

- Fulfilment of the revenue requirement, an accounting technique which sees sufficient revenues to cover operating costs and a reasonable return to capital
- Understandability and feasibility of application
- Stability over time
- Efficient use of resources
- Economic and regional development objectives

Whether this way of calculating rates is a perfect substitute for pricing at the margin, or whether calculation of the marginal cost itself is too difficult, is subject to question.

Offshore Oil and Gas: A Note

The presence of oil and gas reserves in Atlantic Canada has long been known. Closely related deposits of coal are widespread, and extend under the sea off eastern Cape Breton. There has been a single producing oil well at Stoney Brook, New Brunswick, since the early part of the century. Large oil shale deposits in southern New Brunswick await suitable technology to allow commercial extraction.

Attention turned to offshore oil and gas exploration in the late 1950s, with seismic surveys to explore structures around Sable Island on the Scotian Shelf. By 1965, much of the area of the shelf was leased. An exploration well was drilled on the Grand Banks off Newfoundland in 1966, followed by one on Sable Island in 1967. Almost 200 wells have been drilled since this time, mostly in the late 1970s and early 1980s, on the Scotian Shelf, the Grand Banks, the northeastern Newfoundland Shelf, and on the Labrador Shelf as far north as Davis Strait. After 1980, there was a surge of exploration supported by generous federal grants under the Petroleum Incentives Program, which was phased out beginning in 1985. Significant deposits of oil and gas have been identified at several locations.

Development of these reserves must await a suitable mixture of quite high and stable oil prices. Much exploration occurred when the price of oil was artificially high, set by the members of the Organization of Petroleum Exporting Countries. These high prices, however, reduced demand for energy, and induced more exploration for oil all over the world. Disarray within OPEC itself saw prices of oil plunge in 1986, dipping below US$10 per barrel at one point from an historical high of US$35 in the early 1980s.

The economics of oil production comprise three main phases. Exploration is fairly small in the total scheme of things, but has brought significant benefits to the region. Drilling rigs must be serviced and maintained by a fleet of supply vessels. Both rigs and vessels require crews, and local shipyards can obtain some work. One model of the exploration phase off Newfoundland estimated total employment from 809 to 4,822 person-years, or from 1,043 to 7,651 jobs. Associated wages and salaries range from $28 million to $182 million annually, with variations being based on the actual scale of operations at any one time.[3]

Largest benefits will come with development of an oil or gas well. This will vary according to type of deposit, and to chosen method of extraction. Oil can either be extracted by a floating system of production platforms, or by platforms that sit on the ocean floor. Both must be built, and the latter especially must be built close to point of extraction. This means jobs on shore in fabrication yards. Pipelines must be built to take gas ashore, and receiving areas prepared at point of landing. Further pipeline systems are required to take the gas to final market. There is potential at this stage to develop onshore industry based on offshore hydrocarbon production, either using the energy as an input to a wide variety of industrial enterprise, or using it as a material input in production of such commodities as petrochemicals or plastics.

Much, indeed, depends on the success of building a localised industrial base to ensure that jobs do not leave an area once development is finished, and all the commercially feasible reserves in an area are producing. Actual production itself can occur with a much lower level of employment, although trade in hydrocarbons will continue to bring export earnings to the area of production and governments will continue to reap benefits in the form of taxes and royalties.

Summary

The demand for energy in all its forms increases as the full range of economic activity increases, but usually at a faster rate. In Atlantic Canada, energy has been developed to provide power within the region and for export. The variety of energy sources is wide and there are constant experiments and explorations to diversify further.

New developments will see expansion of established methods of generating electricity, including big new hydro works in remote places. There will also be production of oil and gas from reserves off the shores of both Nova Scotia and Newfoundland. All such work will offer a secure supply of energy both for domestic markets and for export.

Footnotes

1. A calorie is the amount of heat required to raise the temperature of one kilogram of water by 1 degree celsius. Its imperial equivalent is the British thermal unit (Btu), or the amount of heat required to raise the temperature of one pound of water by 1 degree Fahrenheit. These estimates, and others, are in A.K. Biswas, *Energy and the Environment*, Energy, Mines and Resources Canada, Ottawa, 1974.

2. Electric *power* (a stock) is measured in watts; a kilowatt (kW) is 1000 watts, a megawatt (MW) is 1000 kW, and a gigawatt (GW) is 1000 MW. Electric *energy* (a flow) is measured in watt-hours, with similar multiples designated kWh, MWh, and GWh. Energy is sometimes referred to as *primary* (the available energy content of the natural resource); *secondary* (the amount delivered to point of final consumption, or primary less the amount lost in conversion and in process of supply); or *tertiary* (the energy in actual final use, or secondary less losses at final end use).

3. Newfoundland and Labrador Petroleum Directorate, *Direct Economic Impact of Total Drilling Activity 1981-1990.* Planning Report Number One, St John's, 1982.

Further Reading

Economic Council of Canada, *Connections: An Energy Strategy for the Future*. Ottawa, 1985.

Energy Mines and Resources Canada, *Electric Power in Canada*. Ottawa, annual. National Energy Board, Canadian Energy: Supply and Demand 1985-2005. Technical Report, Ottawa, 1986.

Voyer, R., *Offshore Oil: Opportunities for Industrial Development and Job Creation*. Canadian Institute for Economic Policy, Industrial Strategy Series. Toronto: James Lorimer and Company, 1983.

CHAPTER 8

Manufacturing: Adding Value to Resources

Manufacturing in Atlantic Canada is heavily integrated with resource production, so discussion in this chapter follows closely from previous sections. Of particular importance is the processing of primary output of the agricultural, fishery, and forest sectors, with some further manufacture of mineral products.

Manufacturing involves the transformation of raw materials into higher-value products by combining them with other material inputs, capital, and labour. The actual amount of value added by the process of manufacture can vary, depending on whether final output is subject to further manufacture into yet higher-value items. For example, manufacture of iron ore into sheet steel may just be one step to the final production of a car or a refrigerator, or some other consumer product. Although the steel is worth more than the iron ore, it is worth less than the final product. In general, most manufactured products in Atlantic Canada are material inputs for further manufacture, often in distant locations. This means that much of the value added to processing the region's resources may benefit areas other than Atlantic Canada.

Manufacturing employment in the region increased from less than 62,500 in 1961 to more than 92,500 at its peak in 1979 (Figure 8.1). There was then a sharp drop in the recession of the early 1980s, and

FIGURE 8.1: MANUFACTURING EMPLOYMENT, ATLANTIC PROVINCES, 1961–1984

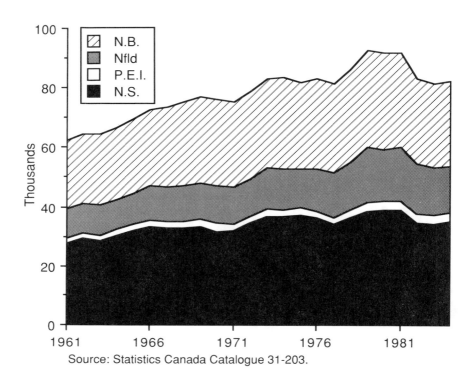

Source: Statistics Canada Catalogue 31-203.

TABLE 8.1: DATA ON SELECTED PRINCIPAL MANUFACTURING INDUSTRIES, ATLANTIC CANADA, 1984

	Establishments	Employment	Wages Paid	Value of Shipments
			– $ million –	
Pulp and paper mills[1]	19	7,967	214	1,294
Fish products	292	16,810	236	1,042
Meat and meat products	24	802	18	175
Sawmills and planing mills	261	3,261	51	257
Breweries[1]	7	748	21	155
All manufacturing	1,994	82,425	1,781	10,147

Note 1) For 1982. Figures after this year are suppressed for reasons of company confidentiality.

Source: Statistics Canada Catalogue 31-203.

FIGURE 8.2: PROPORTIONATE BREAKDOWN OF MANUFACTURING ESTABLISHMENTS BY NUMBER OF EMPLOYEES [1] AND TOTAL EMPLOYEES AS PROPORTION BY SIZE OF EMPLOYMENT AT MANUFACTURING ESTABLISHMENTS [2], ATLANTIC PROVINCES AND CANADA, 1982

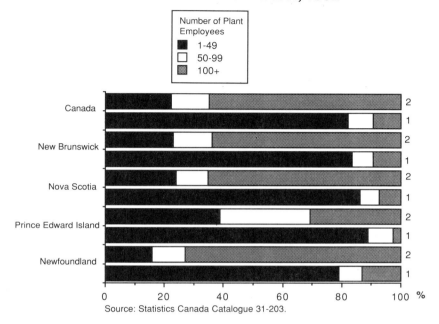

Source: Statistics Canada Catalogue 31-203.

there has not been full recovery to 1979 levels even by mid-decade. Rate of growth in manufacturing employment from 1961 to 1984 was 1.2% each year on average, slightly better than a national rate of 1.1%. Value of goods shipped over the same period increased from less than $1 billion to more than $10 billion, for an annual average rate of increase of almost 11%; inflation over the same period was between 6% and 7% each year (Table 8.1).

Most manufacturing jobs are in relatively few large plants that employ 100 people or more. A large majority of actual plants in Atlantic Canada, however, employ far fewer than 100 workers (Figure 8.2). In Newfoundland, large establishments were less than 14% of all establishments, but had 72.5% of all manufacturing employment. Prince Edward Island diverges a little from this pattern, with a higher incidence of smaller factories accounting for a bigger share of total employment. Both Nova Scotia and New Brunswick adhere quite closely to the national average, with bigger plants accounting for between 50% and 60% of all manufacturing jobs.

TABLE 8.2: MANUFACTURING INDUSTRIES: SOME PROVINCIAL DETAILS 1984

	Employment		Value of Shipments	
	Number	% of Total	$ million	% of Total
Newfoundland and Labrador:				
Fish products	8,637	54.3	401	34.3
Total	15,907	100.0	1,170	100.0
Prince Edward Island:				
Dairy products	352	11.9	69	23.9
Fish products	712	24.0	52	18.0
Total	2,963	100.0	289	100.0
Nova Scotia:				
Pulp and paper products	2,993	8.5	434	9.4
Fish products	5,793	16.5	389	8.5
Dairy products	1,172	3.3	156	3.4
Total	35,024	100.0	4,595	100.0
New Brunswick:				
Pulp and paper products	5,738	20.1	1,021	25.0
Sawmills and planing mills	2,245	7.9	185	4.5
Fish products	3,829	13.4	200	4.9
Total	28,531	100.0	4,092	100.0

Note: These figures relate only to those industries for which information can be published without contravening confidentiality requirements as specified in the Statistics Act. Where an industry is represented by less than five plants in a province, such restrictions apply.

Source: Statistics Canada Catalogue 31-203.

Atlantic manufacturing tends to be smaller scale than nationally. Manufacturing employment stands at about 12% of all employment in Newfoundland in the mid-1980s, about 7% in Prince Edward Island, 12%-13% in Nova Scotia, and about 14% in New Brunswick. In employment as in contribution to gross domestic product, manufacturing is proportionally more important at the national level (18% of all jobs, 21% of gross domestic product).

Manufacturing in Newfoundland is heavily based on fish processing and newsprint production, accounting for some 60% of shipments (Table 8.2). Prince Edward Island depends largely on food processing, both fish and agricultural products. The reliance in New Brunswick falls mainly on forest products and food processing. Even though there is a little more diversity in Nova Scotia's manufacturing, fish processing and pulp and paper products still dominate. Other important manufacturing enterprise in the region includes petroleum refining, ship- and boat-building and repair, steel rail manufacture, and tire production.

The high reliance of Atlantic manufacturing on resource processing brings problems related to seasonality, especially where fish and agricultural products are involved. Overcapacity and higher overhead costs occur as plants must usually be geared towards peak flows of inputs. Problems with seasonality are keenest in single-industry communities scattered throughout the region.

This heavy concentration on a few industries should not obscure the fact that there is a wide variety of other manufacturing enterprise in Atlantic Canada. Often, this provides inputs to other industry nearby, such as small machine shops, construction supply operations (ready-mix concrete, bricks or lumber, for example). There are also pockets of "high-tech" industries producing electronic equipment, medical equipment and supplies, and navigational or radio-transmitter products. Textiles and clothing plants (both specialised and mass-production), crafts, furniture, aerospace component factories are some of the other industries.

High-tech industries in the region usually have a few things in common. The high value of their final output means they are more footloose and need not locate as close to market as lower value production. Location decisions, therefore, can accommodate the whims or fancies of the people who begin the companies. Production can occur in places a fair distance from final market, given reasonable access to these markets. Transportation costs themselves are less of a burden because of the higher value of the end-product.

A final aspect of Atlantic manufacturing is the high degree of Canadian ownership, although this varies from sector to sector and between provinces. Canadian ownership accounts for about 80% of manufacturing employment in Newfoundland, 66% in Nova Scotia, and 81% in New Brunswick. In Ontario, Canadian ownership accounts for about 50%. Patterns in Atlantic Canada must be qualified by the fact that ownership of important resource processing capacity (principally pulp and paper mills) is substantially non-Canadian, especially in Nova Scotia and New Brunswick.

Some Further Aspects of Atlantic Manufacturing

Efforts to diversify Atlantic manufacturing have been widespread but of limited success. Much higher-value Canadian manufacture remains concentrated in Ontario, as can be demonstrated by use of a simple location

FIGURE 8.3: LOCATION QUOTIENTS FOR MANUFACTURING BY REGION IN CANADA SELECTED YEARS, 1870–1984

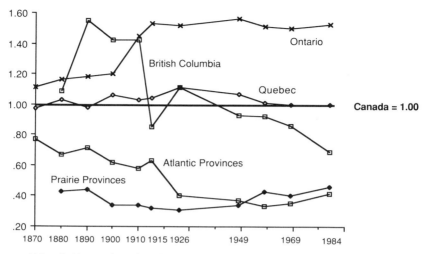

Notes: 1) Measured as value-added per person in each region as ratio of national average.
2) Note that the time series is not discrete after 1910.
Source: H.M. Pinchin *The Regional Impact of the Canadian Tariff* , Economic Council of Canada, 1979, updated from Statistics Canada Catalogue 31-203.

quotient (Figure 8.3). Plotting the quotient over a number of years shows the steady decline of concentration of manufacturing in Atlantic Canada, with a particularly sharp drop between 1915 and 1926. As Atlantic manufacturing has gone down and stayed down, that in Ontario has gone up and stayed up almost as a direct inverse. A slight narrowing of the gap since 1959 coincides with the first real federal attempt to implement regionally-specific industrial policies, coupled with substantial expansion of resource-based processing in Atlantic Canada.

Although many things can be invoked to explain this disparity in manufacturing concentration — seasonality, size of local markets, length of production runs, higher-value products — one is important but rather elusive: entrepreneurship. This hard-to-quantify factor is acknowledged as vital in industrial success. Usually it must be combined with other elements of production (resources and capital especially) but is more difficult to identify. Emigration of people from the region since 1945 probably took some of the most enterprising minds to other parts; many senior managers and executives in some of Canada's most successful corporations can lay claim to an Atlantic upbringing, but have usually had to leave the region to attain success.

Atlantic Canada Today

There are notable examples of great success in the Atlantic region. Most of them owe their origins to family ownership of resources or establishment of a store. Diversification and expansion from this base has come at various speeds, but has usually been quite modest. Family-owned concerns now embrace oil refining, resource extraction and processing, far-flung retail empires, transportation, and financial services. Many of the best-known enterprises still maintain corporate headquarters within the region, although operations may spread across Canada and around the world. Some have encountered solid success within the region, only to be bought by outside interests and moved away; others have moved away by their own choice to be closer to bigger markets. Those who have stayed may have done so only on the strength of family ties and the fact that this is where their industry first began.

The value of these industries moves beyond the value of actual production. It is argued that they are less likely to buckle during recession, unlike "branch plant" industries. This sense of responsibility to local communities, in turn, promotes a loyal workforce, which will occasionally make sacrifices on behalf of the company. The cohesion and integrity of the community is thereby enhanced.

Summary

Although Atlantic Canada's manufacturing relies heavily on resource processing, this should not obscure the wide diversity of other, smaller scale industries that operate in the region. Many of the factories are small, although the few that employ larger numbers of people account for a disproportionate share of total manufacturing employment.

There are occasional surprises. Some manufacturing enterprises rely more on personal preferences than strict economic dictates for locational decisions. The higher value of their end products offsets the higher costs of selling in a wide array of markets. As well, there are notable examples of national and international manufacturing firms, many of which began modestly and expanded as markets have allowed. These are of particular value in local communities where they may be major employers.

Further Reading

Statistics Canada, *Manufacturing Industries of Canada: National and Provincial Areas*. Ottawa, annual.

Zohar, U., *Canadian Manufacturing: A Study in Productivity and Technological Change*. Industrial Strategy Series, Canadian Institute for Economic Policy. Two volumes. Ottawa,1982.

CHAPTER 9

Investment: To Stay Competitive

Investment is a measure of renewal and expansion of an economy's productive capacity. As such, it can help sustain continued economic progress or, if not undertaken, can prevent a society from realising its potential.

Investment requires capital, but equally helps generate more capital in the form of equity. A consumer buying a house is an investor, as he expects his equity in that property to increase. Investment in industry increases capital stock in that industry, allowing modernisation of plant and equipment. These, in turn, stimulate increases in productivity and make the industry more competitive and efficient. Investment also allows industries to absorb technological developments.

Atlantic Investment Trends

Capital formation per person in Atlantic Canada increased at an annual average rate of about 10% between 1961 and 1984 (Figure 9.1). This compares with an 8.7% rate nationally, and an inflation rate of about 6% over the same period. Examination of the different types of capital formation indicates changes. Government capital spending has taken up a progressively smaller proportion of all investment, while private investment in the region's housing stock has increased markedly, especially since the mid-1970s. This coincides nicely with successive cohorts of "baby-boomers" entering the labour force, settling down, and buying a home. General prosperity and two-income families have stimulated household formation.

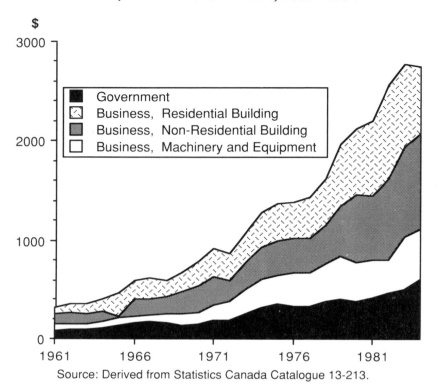

FIGURE 9.1: CAPITAL FORMATION PER PERSON BY TYPE, ATLANTIC CANADA, 1961–1984

$

- ■ Government
- ▨ Business, Residential Building
- ▦ Business, Non-Residential Building
- □ Business, Machinery and Equipment

Source: Derived from Statistics Canada Catalogue 13-213.

Residential investment contributes both to the equity of individuals as property values increase, and to the profitability of industries that build the homes. Business non-residential investment, and spending on machinery and equipment add to an economy's productive capacity. Both have increased markedly since 1971, and not all of the increase is due to inflation. A significant part of the increase has been in the form of big electrical generating works, which have given especially big boosts to investment spending per person in Newfoundland and New Brunswick at different times.

A higher dependence on public investment in the region's capital formation reflects, to a degree, the workings of capital markets in Canada. Access to equity capital is dictated largely by stock markets in parts of the country away from the Atlantic provinces. This means that private and corporate savings from the region are more likely to be used to invest in other parts of the country.

Investment and Productivity

Increases in productivity are a vital part of overall economic progress. They are important because the more efficiently an economy can produce a given set of items, the more competitive it will be in available markets. Productivity increases allow a more rapid accumulation of wealth or equity, thereby permitting some members of society to consume more without doing so at the expense of others. Increases in productivity, in other words, allow the economic "pie" to get bigger.

There is disagreement over the best way to measure productivity, which in general terms denotes the use of a given set of inputs to produce a marketable commodity or service. Increases in productivity, therefore, achieve an increase in output by a less than proportional increase in application or combination of inputs. Productivity itself has traditonally been expressed in terms of output per worker; this is technically labour productivity, which should be distinguished from total factor productivity. This refers to the efficiency with which all inputs (labour, capital, equipment, management skills) are combined to produce output.

It is difficult to measure increases in productivity. Industries vary in input, equipment and labour skills required, and in value-added during manufacture of end product. Some industries lend themselves more easily to installation of better equipment because of homogeneity of raw materials or of final output. Others must deal with quite a diverse set of inputs (fish, for example, vary widely in terms of size and biological composition) that cannot be adapted to automation easily.

Some Measurements of Manufacturing Productivity

Value of manufacturing shipments per worker in Atlantic manufacturing plants fell short of the national average by between 10 and 20 percentage points in the years up to 1971 (Figure 9.2). There was a sustained increase in the years up to 1974, followed by several years when the regional average was either close to or exceeded the national average. However, there has been a sharp decline to earlier levels since 1982.

If productivity is measured as value-added per production-hour paid, however, Atlantic Canada falls far short of the Canadian average; there was a range in 1984 from 52% of the national average in Prince Edward Island, to 89% in Nova Scotia, with Newfoundland at 55% and New Brunswick at 75% (Figure 9.3). This disparity should not reflect negatively on the region's labour force. Productivity depends on a number of factors, such as industrial structure, capital stock, the rate of adoption of new technology, management skills, and scale of operation.

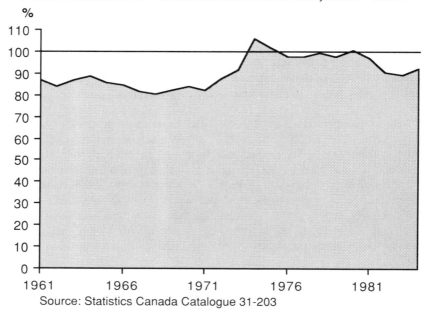

FIGURE 9.2: VALUE OF MANUFACTURING SHIPMENTS PER EMPLOYEE, ATLANTIC CANADA AS A PROPORTION OF CANADIAN AVERAGE, 1961–1984

Source: Statistics Canada Catalogue 31-203

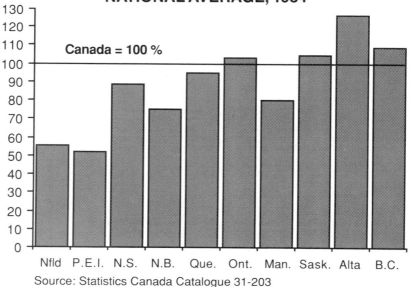

FIGURE 9.3: VALUE-ADDED PER PRODUCTIVITY-HOUR PAID, ALL PROVINCES AS A PROPORTION OF THE NATIONAL AVERAGE, 1984

Source: Statistics Canada Catalogue 31-203

FIGURE 9.4: CUMULATIVE PERCENTAGE CHANGES IN VALUE OF CONSTRUCTION AND GROSS DOMESTIC PRODUCT, ATLANTIC CANADA, 1961–1985 (CONSTANT TERMS)

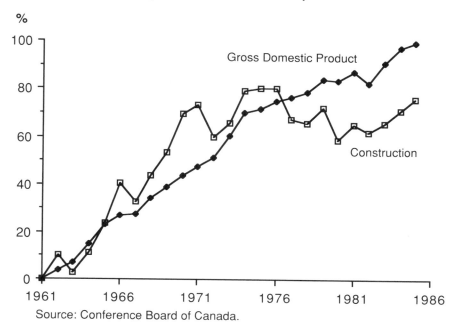

Source: Conference Board of Canada.

TABLE 9.1: VALUE OF CONSTRUCTION, ATLANTIC PROVINCES AND CANADA, 1971, 1981 AND 1986

	1971	1981	1986
	– millions of dollars –		
Newfoundland and Labrador	552.8	1,034.5	1,426.4
Prince Edward Island	61.2	153.6	229.6
Nova Scotia	452.8	1,305.2	1,965.8
New Brunswick	351.9	1,022.3	1,262.8
Atlantic Canada	1,418.7	3,515.6	4,884.6
Canada	15,865.3	48,327.0	63,822.3
Atlantic Canada as % of Canada	8.9%	7.8%	7.7%

Source: Statistics Canada Catalogue 64-201

Some industries in Atlantic Canada (for example, pulp and paper man-ufacture) are globally competitive, reflecting high levels of productivity in plants. In other respects, however, industrial structure falls far short of North American standards. Fish processing in Atlantic Canada, for exam-ple, is an important industry, yet productivity can be demonstrated to be only about one-third or one-half that of American plants. American plants concentrate much more on production of higher-value, consumer-ready end products, whereas in Atlantic plants there is substantial output of lower-value fish blocks, which receive more processing elsewhere.

This inability to specialise within an industry in Atlantic Canada has hindered productivity growth. Other inhibiting factors include generally lower levels of education and training (aggravated once again by emigra-tion of the "brightest and the best"), causing a particularly serious shortfall at the managerial level; slower rates of adoption of new techniques of production or improved technologies; and a more scattered, less urban population distribution, which inhibits development of "agglomeration" economies of scale.

Investment and the Construction Industry

The construction industry has developed around decisions to invest, and prospers more or less in line with investment intentions. Ups and downs in the construction cycle, therefore, have close relationships with ups and downs in overall economic activity, especially changes in interest rates. The cycles themselves may not coincide exactly with wider economic fluctuations; for example, big projects may begin during good times, but as they take such a long time to complete are quite likely to extend through recessions.

Construction output in Atlantic Canada since 1961 has been both erratic from year to year, and has formed a declining part of overall gross domestic product. An uneven climb to a peak in 1970-1971 coincided with a great deal of infrastructure developments (roads and so on) linked to a flurry of development in provincial transportation networks. Since the mid-1970s (a period characterised by high interest rates) construction activity has lagged behind overall increases in gross domestic product (Figure 9.4); it still had a value of output at a little less than $5 billion in 1986 (Table 9.1).

Construction remains an important source of jobs, and employed almost 50,000 people in 1986. As with the industry generally, this number can vary widely (Figure 9.5). There is also a seasonal effect that sees less building going on during winter months. Insecurity of employment is compensated in part by higher than average wages, $510 a week com-pared with an industrial aggregate average of $430.

110

FIGURE 9.5: CONSTRUCTION EMPLOYMENT, ATLANTIC CANADA, 1971–1986

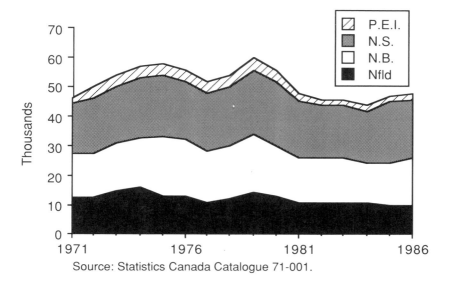

Source: Statistics Canada Catalogue 71-001.

There are two broad parts to the construction industry. Building construction includes residential, industrial, commercial and most institutional/governmental work, buildings in which people live or work. Engineering construction includes a variety of heavy or civil works such as roads, airports, waterworks, dams, electricity stations, and marine works. Building construction firms vary widely in size, with many smaller companies involved in constructing homes. Engineering construction is more often the domain of much bigger, national or international companies.

Summary

The importance of investment as a generator of economic growth cannot be underestimated. In this respect, capital formation in Atlantic Canada has increased substantially since the 1960s, mostly as a series of big projects have come and gone. The region's electricity generating capacity has increased markedly in consequence, as has overall infrastructure and housing stock.

Atlantic Canada has some difficulties with respect to investment. Access to capital is more difficult, with much private equity (including private and corporate savings) being channelled through stock markets to enterprises in other parts of Canada. A higher emphasis on resource industries implies less capability to increase productivity by means of investment.

Industrial productivity, therefore, lags behind national levels, and is less likely to increase as fast under existing industrial structures.

Further Reading

Auer, L., *Regional Disparities of Productivity and Growth in Canada*. Prepared for the Economic Council of Canada. Ottawa, 1979.

Economic Council of Canada, *Living Together: A Study of Regional Disparities*. Ottawa, 1977. Especially Chapter 6.

Economic Council of Canada, *Newfoundland: From Dependency to Self-Reliance*. Ottawa, 1980. Especially Chapter 2.

Postner, H.H. and L. Wesa, *Canadian Productivity Growth: An Alternative (Input-Output) Analysis*. Prepared for the Economic Council of Canada. Ottawa, 1983.

CHAPTER 10

Regional Development: The Pursuit of Parity

Regional concerns and interests are integral parts of the Canadian economic and political union. They could be described as either the signs of a healthy democratic process at work, or the shrill squabbling of a family of fractious siblings. All stages in building the present confederation of ten provinces have had to accommodate regional concerns, with explicit or implicit guarantees. Policies to address regional issues have encompassed transportation, resources, tariffs, and social and industrial programs.

Measures of Regional Disparity

Since the 1950s, there has been a wide range of initiatives to address regional economic disparities. Such inequalities have been seen most frequently in Atlantic Canada; in spite of the best efforts, they have persisted. Many examples have already been encountered in this book. Productivity is lower, as are measures of capital formation. Education levels tend to be lower partly because many of the better educated Atlantic Canadians have left to pursue opportunities elsewhere. A long record of net emigration from the region itself, indeed, is a reflection of regional disparity. As one report noted almost 50 years ago: Economically, Canada can be compared to a string of beads, and they are not all pearls.[1]

The persistence of disparities can be shown in terms of personal income per person for the principal regions of Canada (Figure 10.1). This measures all the different types of income, both earned and "unearned"

FIGURE 10.1: PERSONAL INCOME PER PERSON BY
REGION, AS A PERCENTAGE OF CANADA, 1926–1984

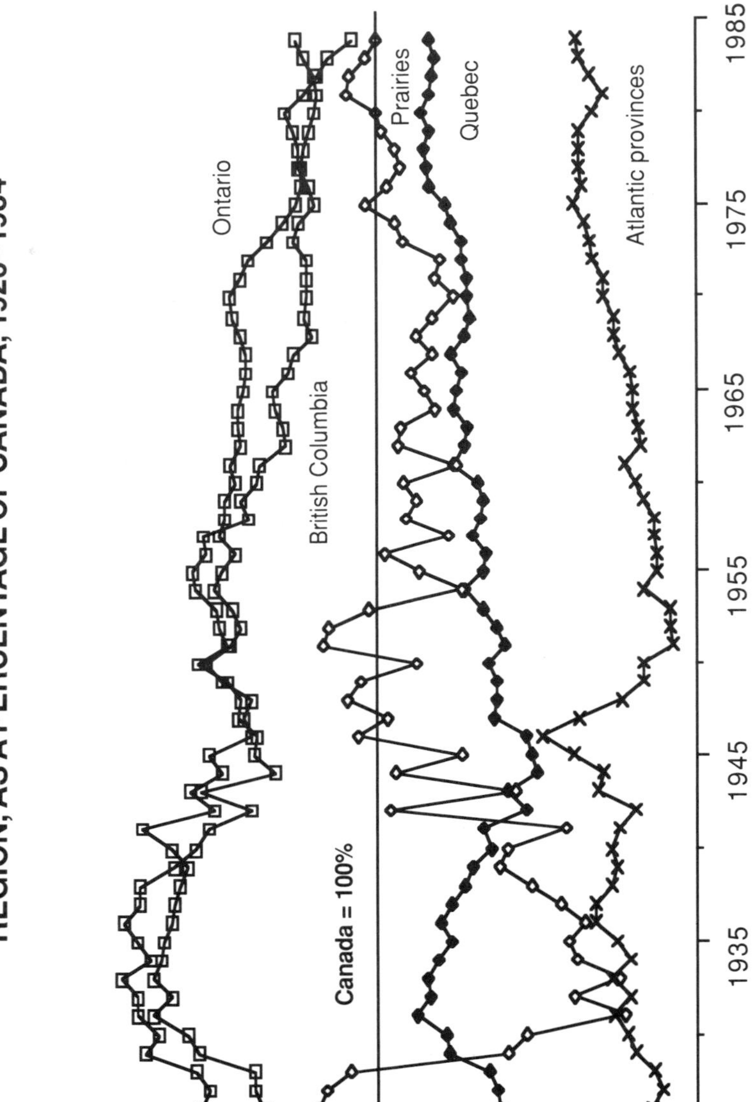

Source: Statistics Canada 13-213.

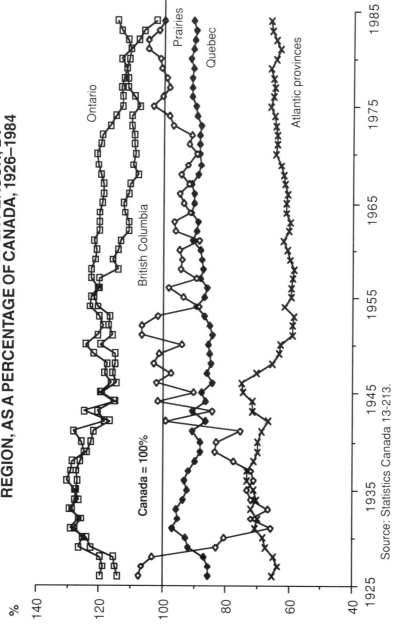

FIGURE 10.2: EARNED INCOME PER PERSON, BY REGION, AS A PERCENTAGE OF CANADA, 1926–1984

Ontario

Prairies

Quebec

British Columbia

Canada = 100%

Atlantic provinces

Source: Statistics Canada 13-213.

FIGURE 10.3: UNEMPLOYMENT RATE, ATLANTIC CANADA AND CANADA, 1954–1986

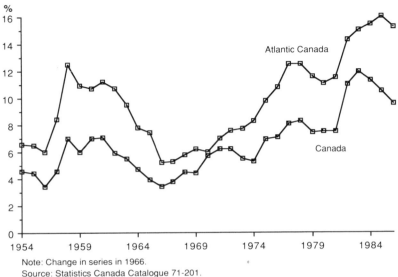

Note: Change in series in 1966.
Source: Statistics Canada Catalogue 71-201.

(mainly transfer payments from various levels of government, including pensions, unemployment benefits, social assistance, industrial incentives) expressed as a percentage of the national average since 1926. By this measure, Atlantic Canada has persistently been lowest in Canada. Prairie incomes were close in the early 1930s, and in fact dipped below Atlantic incomes in 1931 and 1933 during the worst of the Great Depression. There was improvement during the Second World War, but this was followed by a profound slump from 1946 to 1951; this was aggravated to a degree when Newfoundland joined Canada in 1949. A gradual improvement since the early 1950s can be attributed substantially to the rise of transfer payments as Canada's social welfare system developed, and to an array of regional industrial incentives since the early 1960s.

A striking feature of Figure 10.1 is that average incomes in the principal regions of Canada have tended to converge towards the national average with the exception of those in Atlantic Canada. The line in the diagram denoting incomes in Atlantic Canada has remained stubbornly low and flat. Even this low average for the region masks wide variations both between the four provinces and within each province. Personal income per person in Nova Scotia in 1984 was 81% of the national average, the highest in the region. New Brunswick and Prince Edward Island stood at 74 and 72% respectively, while Newfoundland stood at 67%.

116

Adjusting the data to exclude such sources of income as transfer and incentive payments allows us to examine earned income per person (Figure 10.2). Once again, Atlantic Canada is at the bottom of the pile, only more profoundly so since the late 1940s up to the present. In 1984, earned income per person in the region was 66% of the national average; in 1926 it stood at 65.2%. Total personal income per person (both earned and unearned) in the mid-1980s is a rather more respectable 75% of the national average.

There are other measures of disparity. Unemployment rates are higher in Atlantic Canada; they have usually become disproportionately higher during recessions (for example during the late 1950s, mid-1970s, and early 1980s), and have been slower to come down during recoveries (Figure 10.3). After the 1982 recession, the Canadian rate began declining in 1984; it took two more years for the Atlantic rate to show any improvement. Participation rates in the Atlantic provinces are lower than the national average, and transfers from governments to individuals, businesses, and other governments are higher (Table 10.1). Provincial output (as measured by gross domestic product) is lower, and a bigger proportion of this is accounted for directly by public administration and defence spending.

Theories of Regional Development [2]

Theories to explain regional disparities draw on several different economic theories with universal and more general application. The staples approach, for example, emphasises a region's endowment of marketable resources. As the availability and marketability of a given known resource base varies, so does the regional economy. Variations in demand for fish, lumber and coal can explain at least part of the ups and downs of the Atlantic economy during its history.

Reduced demand for any staple product will cause a drop in labour demand and wages, with eventual high unemployment and emigration. The adjustment may take several decades. This can be avoided by successive discoveries of new, more marketable resources such as oil in Alberta or lumber in British Columbia, which absorb surplus labour and may even stimulate immigration. An alternative is to subsidise production within the region of those products which would, without the subsidy, not be marketable outside the region. This may be replaced or supplemented by subsidising transportation costs to market.

The staples approach explains differentials in employment creation to a degree, but its reliance on a resource endowment as prime determinant of regional growth is faulty. It does not, for example, explain the success

TABLE 10.1: MEASUREMENTS OF DISPARITY AND DEPENDENCE, ATLANTIC PROVINCES 1971, 1976, 1981, AND 1984

	Newfoundland and Labrador	Prince Edward Island	Nova Scotia	New Brunswick	Canada
Gdp per person as % of national:					
1971	56.2	52.3	67.9	63.7	100.0
1976	53.8	52.4	66.3	64.0	100.0
1981	52.0	50.5	61.3	63.1	100.0
1984	59.5	56.3	68.9	65.0	100.0
Participation rate (percent):					
1971	45.0	54.3	52.2	49.8	58.1
1976	49.4	56.7	55.2	53.6	61.5
1981	53.1	59.1	57.8	53.6	64.7
1984	52.9	60.2	59.3	55.1	64.8
Dependency ratio[1]					
1971	1.48	1.06	1.02	1.14	0.82
1976	1.35	0.97	1.00	1.10	0.75
1981	1.19	0.90	0.92	0.99	0.67
1984	1.37	0.90	0.94	1.13	0.74
Total personal transfers per person as % of national average:					
1971	133.2	114.6	102.9	104.2	100.0
1976	150.1	121.8	107.4	118.5	100.0
1981	144.9	126.6	109.8	116.7	100.0
1984	137.8	127.4	103.5	112.7	100.0
UIC payments per person as % of national average:					
1971	148.8	109.8	119.5	134.2	100.0
1976	224.8	186.9	127.6	184.1	100.0
1981	260.0	216.5	141.0	205.0	100.0
1984	216.7	197.3	120.7	173.9	100.0
Public administration and defence as % of gdp:					
1971	9.1	18.9	17.8	15.8	7.3
1976	9.9	21.8	15.8	11.2	7.1
1981	11.7	20.4	15.1	14.5	6.8
1984	12.0	19.6	13.8	11.6	6.9

Note: 1) Number of people 15 and older who are not working divided by number of people 15 and older who are working.

Source: Statistics Canada Catalogue 13-001, 13-213, 71-201; the Conference Board of Canada.

Atlantic Canada Today

of resource-poor economies such as Switzerland or Japan. An extension of this approach invokes theories in developmental economics, a body of analysis that seeks to explain why some countries are poor, others rich. To reduce these disparities, the usual approaches have been to emphasise capital accumulation, infrastructure development, agricultural development in the less-developed parts of the world. Although certain parts of the developmental approach have an appeal in explaining the relative backwardness of Atlantic Canada, it does not explain such things as the relatively small part agriculture plays in the region compared to Third World countries, and the relatively comfortable lifestyles of most people in Atlantic Canada.

A large body of economic thought is couched in neoclassical theory. This does not explicitly accommodate differences in regional development, but emphasises more flexibility of prices and wages, and the mobility of principal factors of production such as capital and labour. Unemployment, for example, arises from the market's failure to equate labour supply and demand and requires the price of labour (wages) to come down to redress this inequality. It also offers the unemployed the opportunity to move to where wages are higher and jobs exist. Their departure will both raise income in the sending region and lower it in the receiving region and eventually equalise differentials.

The Keynesian approach attempts to make the neoclassical adjustment period shorter by government intervention in the management of aggregate demand to modify market forces. Its application to parts (regions or industries) rather than the whole (a national economy) is dubious, however, especially when the tools of management (such as fiscal or monetary policy) can only be effectively applied at the level of the whole. Parts of the whole, as well, differ widely in terms of important factors, such as productivity and incomes, which are not adequately accommodated by this approach.

Several strands of the various approaches have been brought together into a body of knowledge referred to as regional science. This attempts to inject a spatial or locational element into investment decisions with corresponding emphasis on transportation costs and the geographical variation in labour and material costs. Population and settlement patterns are important to regional scientists, and allow them to identify concentrations of such things as economies of scale, of localisation, and of urbanisation. Growth poles may emerge, and exports from the immediate region are stressed, although critics assert that this should not be at the expense of other relative forces such as wages and prices.

Defining Regional Policy

This brief assessment of theory serves to underline the fact that regional development policies must try to reconcile constitutional rights of equality of opportunity with economic realities. In the absence of explicit regional policies, this reconciliation is left to market forces, which assume mobile factors of production. Equality of opportunity is maintained by a mobile labour force, which allows free movement both between industries and regions.

This process rarely moves fast enough to avoid unacceptable social and political costs in an advanced society such as Canada's. Implicit and explicit policies have arisen, therefore, to ensure that all parts of the country participate in the benefits of economic progress. This has been a difficult goal to achieve even in countries with a more compact geographical configuration than Canada.

Even generalising regional differentiation along provincial lines does not simplify the task of achieving equitable economic growth. Sub-provincial areas even in Canada's smallest provinces frequently fall far short of provincial standards of prosperity and development. If such areas cannot even aspire to provincial levels of income and employment, which themselves fall short of national standards, the total problem is greatly aggravated.

Full participation of all regions in national growth and well-being also requires an effort on the part of the provinces to contribute to that growth. This, in turn, requires reduction of disparities that exist between regions as a first step, and the fullest use of resources (both physical and human) as a second step. To achieve the first of these would require advances in productivity and incomes at rates appreciably higher than the national average. Policies aimed at these goals have a long, if chequered, history in Canada.

Development of Regional Policies

Confederation in 1867 was a response in British North America to threats from outside. The United States abandoned reciprocity in retaliation for Britain's support of the South during the Civil War, and as Reconstruction began; Britain itself extended its adopted course of free trade by abandoning imperial preference in trade. Movement towards unity between the Canadas, Nova Scotia and New Brunswick was an obvious response. This unity was not achieved without dissent in the regions. To ignore these regional feelings since 1867 has always been politically dangerous.

Regional policy at first was couched in terms of the Canadian tariff and transportation policy. The tariff allowed the development of manufacturing industries, and artificially low rail freight rates enabled the peripheries of the country to compete in important central markets, since natural north-south trade routes were distorted by the tariff. Tampering with freight rates in the early part of twentieth century, however, effectively destroyed much Atlantic manufacturing before a concerted response (the Maritimes Rights Movement) emerged in the 1920s. By this time, as well, there was a depression. The Maritime Freight Rates Act emerged from the recommendations of the Duncan Royal Commission in 1928. This restored a measure of competitive access for Maritime products in central markets by subsidising rail rates, and still operates in the late 1980s.

The vulnerability of certain regions was sadly emphasised during the 1930s, however. The Prairies, depending so heavily on a wheat economy, suffered terribly from loss of topsoil. Regional policies emerged; these changed the emphasis from passive transportation development to income support, particularly in rural areas. This so severely taxed the treasuries of several provinces (Alberta was in a de facto state of bankruptcy in 1934) that the Royal Commission on Dominion-Provincial Relations (the Rowell-Sirois Commission) was formed in 1937 to examine the problem.

The Commission reported in 1939, and this report can fairly be regarded as the source of regional policies. One recommendation was for a system of National Adjustment Grants to allow poorer provinces to maintain minimum acceptable standards of services by cash transfers from richer provinces via the federal tax system; this principle of equalisation, indeed, had also been suggested in the Duncan Commission report a decade or so earlier, but did not become a part of federal-provincial relations until 1957. The principal forms of transfers in the mid-1980s account for about 20 cents of each provincial revenue dollar; in Atlantic Canada, this share is between 35 and 50 cents.

Another heritage of the depression years was the beginnings of unemployment insurance in 1941. There was a variety of other measures over the years: conditional grants to provinces for specific purposes such as road-building; hospital insurance; assistance to the aged and disabled; and airport development. A distinction between income maintenance and economic development began to emerge, based in part on the feeling that more of the latter would reduce dependence on the former.

The tariff as principal tool of industrial development had evidently not benefited regions away from southern Ontario. The post-war years saw very bad times in Atlantic Canada as other parts of the country leapt ahead. Gross domestic product in Alberta and British Columbia, for example, increased at an average annual rate of 10.5% and 10.9% respectively between 1945 and 1950; Prince Edward Island and Nova Scotia increased at 4.8% and 4.1% respectively over the same period. Disparities were noted, but were regarded as temporary aberrations that would disappear as national wealth trickled outwards.

North American prosperity reached new heights in the mid-1950s, but the only way Atlantic Canadians could share in this was to leave home. The Royal Commission on Canada's Economic Prospects (the Gordon Commission), which reported in 1957, drew attention to the plight of many people in disadvantaged regions such as Atlantic Canada; indeed, many rural people were living in poverty. A direct result was wider application of parts of the Prairie Farm Rehabilitation Administration of the 1930s, a policy that arose naturally from election of the Diefenbaker government, also in 1957. It was designed to help to ease the disproportionate burden of industrial adjustment which fell on the shoulders of agricultural labourers and small farmers, and was based on experiences in the Prairies in the depression years. The wider concept was the Agricultural Rehabilitation and Development Administration (ARDA) of 1961.

ARDA was intended to improve the lives of small farmers in areas of marginal agriculture. It quickly became evident that the only way this could be achieved was by having fewer small farmers. The challenge then became to find work for those who left the land. This, in turn, led to the realisation that rural and urban economies are closely interrelated. An initiative which sprang directly from ARDA was the Fund for Rural Economic Development in 1966, a broadly-based program for severely distressed rural areas.

Also in the early 1960s, the Atlantic Development Board (ADB), designed to initiate major public works, emerged from the Capital Projects Commission of the Atlantic Provinces. Not only would these works provide employment in their own right, but they would also improve the infrastructure of the region and enable it to share in national prosperity more easily. ADB began operations in 1963, as did the Area Development Agency, designed to assist manufacturing industries. Although the emphasis on manufacturing was appropriate, direction of assistance usually was not; it was aimed at areas of high unemployment to the exclusion of major population centres, where established infrastructure would probably have provided a better chance of success.

Mounting criticism of the various programs emerged towards the end of the 1960s. It came from many quarters, including the Atlantic Provinces Economic Council. There was a lack of focus and some initiatives were inappropriate. The Department of Regional Economic Expansion (DREE) was established in 1969, with a specific mandate to stimulate economic development in the area to the east of Trois-Rivières, Quebec. New programs included the Special Areas Act and the Regional Development Incentives Act.

Concentration of effort on a specific region of Canada (Atlantic Canada and the Gaspé) did not persist. Two events conspired to dilute the effort. The Quebec crisis of 1970 threw the prospect of separation into sharp relief, and more and more development money went to French Canada in an effort to avert this threat. Also, recession around the globe due to higher oil prices inhibited flexibility in applying regional development policies.

The early 1970s saw the beginnings of General Development Agreements (GDAs) which could encompass any number of sub-agreements for specific purposes. Costs of these programs were to be shared between federal and provincial governments. The regional focus was further diluted, however, as agreements were signed with all the provinces except Prince Edward Island, already covered by a 15-year Comprehensive Development Plan which had begun in 1969. Although highly regarded for their cooperative approach, GDAs lacked the political visibility the federal government would have preferred; they were, indeed, perceived to contribute to a round of "province-building" in the late 1970s and early 1980s.

Another change in emphasis occurred in 1982 when DREE was combined with the Department of Industry, Trade and Commerce to form the new Department of Regional Industrial Expansion (DRIE). The Ministry of State for Economic and Regional Development had a coordinating role within the new scheme, but this department was short-lived. The reorganisation was largely prompted by severe cyclical problems, which afflicted central Canada especially; money intended to stimulate structural changes in disadvantaged regions was diverted to overcome these cyclical difficulties. The principal tool for delivery of assistance programs became the Industrial and Regional Development Program (IRDP). Companies anywhere in Canada could apply for assistance, although the level of assistance varied according to a Development Index, calculated to reflect local economic circumstances. GDAs have survived as Economic and Regional Development Agreements with similar purposes but requiring more money from the provinces to implement sub-agreements.

The mid- and late 1980s saw further developments aimed at moving emphasis back to needy regions from the perceived national emphasis embodied in DRIE. The new department remained, but new programs were set up to provide special incentives to Atlantic Canada and particularly to Cape Breton. The Atlantic Enterprise Program had interest rate subsidies and other forms of assistance. The Atlantic Opportunities Program was designed to increase the share of federal purchasing going to Atlantic Canada.

A final development saw creation of the Atlantic Canada Opportunities Agency (ACOA) in 1987. The new agency is intended to put administration and assessment of Atlantic development policies firmly in the hands of those people (Atlantic Canadians) they are designed to assist. This involved movement of most previously mentioned programs from DRIE and to ACOA, to be administered from offices within the region. A five-year commitment exceeding $1 billion is available for operating the agency and providing development money.

Regional Development: An Assessment

It is easy to criticise the regional development policies that have been tried so far. Most criticisms focus on the lack of political will and time (the two are synonymous to a degree) to allow policies to take effect. This has usually seen a shift of effort from the regions the policies are designed to assist, towards a national base.

Demonstration of this trend comes from DREE and DRIE records. Some 53% of departmental spending in the fiscal year 1969/70 (DREE's first year of operation) was in Atlantic Canada (Figure 10.4). In 1981/82 (its last year of operation as a separate department) this proportion was down to less than 32%. The Atlantic share of total spending by DRIE in 1984/85 was 16.1%, compared with 42.6% in Quebec and 23% in Ontario.

There have been other changes in emphasis in national industrial development policies. Defence contracts have become a major source of regional spending. As tariffs around the world have been lowered under successive rounds of the General Agreement on Tariffs and Trade, the Canadian tariff has been replaced as a general tool of industrial development by specific sectoral programs. Emphasis has changed in overall terms from development to adjustment as the aim of industrial policy. Emergence of newly industrialising countries has seen their exports capture larger and larger portions of the internal markets of the industrialised countries. Labour-intensive industries, and older heavy manufacturing, have been particularly vulnerable to this trend, and politicians have been hard put to resist pleas for adjustment assistance or protection from imports.

FIGURE 10.4: SPENDING BY THE DEPARTMENT OF REGIONAL ECONOMIC EXPANSION IN CANADA'S PRINCIPAL REGIONS, 1969–1983

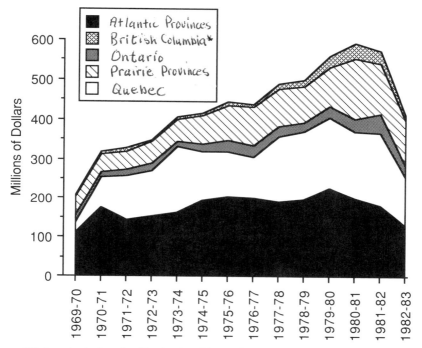

*Notes: Including the Territories. These figures represent commitments and not necessarily actual spending in any one fiscal year. If a commitment for a project was not taken up for any reason, these figures overstate actual spending.

Source: Department of Regional Economic Expansion, Annual Reports.

Several decades of regional development policies in Atlantic Canada have improved the quality of social services, health, education, and infrastructure. Atlantic Canadians have also benefited from access to the prosperity of other parts of Canada, whether manufacturing jobs in Ontario or oil jobs in Alberta. Atlantic Canada still remains at lower levels of development and income, and higher levels of dependence on government spending and transfer, than other parts of the country. In this respect, the region remains underdeveloped.

Footnotes

1. Royal Commission on Dominion-Provincial Relations, *Report*. Ottawa, 1940, p. 186.

2. This section draws on *Living Together: A Study of Regional Disparities* by the Economic Council of Canada, Chapter 3.

Further Reading

Brewis, T.N., *Regional Economic Policies in Canada*. Macmillan Company of Canada, Toronto, 1969.

Coffey, W.J. and M. Polèse (eds.), *Still Living Together: Recent Trends and Future Directions in Canadian Regional Development*. The Institute for Research on Public Policy, Halifax, 1986.

Economic Council of Canada, *Living Together: A Study of Regional Disparities*. Ottawa, 1977.

Forbes, E.R., *Maritime Rights: The Maritime Rights Movement, 1919-1927, A Study in Canadian Regionalism*. McGill-Queen's University Press, Montreal, 1979.

Matthews, R., *The Creation of Regional Dependency*. University of Toronto Press, Toronto, 1983.

Royal Commission on the Economic Union and Development Prospects for Canada, *Report*. Donald S. Macdonald, Chairman, Ottawa, 1985. Especially chapters 9 and 22.

Savoie, D.J., *Regional Economic Development: Canada's Search for Solutions*. University of Toronto Press, Toronto, 1986.

Senate Committee on National Finance, *Government Policy and Regional Development*. D.D. Everett, Chairman, Ottawa, 1982.

CHAPTER 11

Services: The Intangible Economy

Opinions about service industries as economic endeavour vary. Both Adam Smith and Karl Marx regarded them as parasitic, living off the productive and tangible fruits of true economic enterprise. In many centrally planned economies services are accorded the status of a welfare function; they are seen as not contributing to production or the creation of wealth, and are relegated to second place after goods production. This image is reinforced by the inclusion of government in the service sector (frequently an unpopular form of economic activity) and the fact that many service occupations involve low skills and incomes.

This poor reputation has not prevented services from accounting for almost 70% of the value of all economic production in Atlantic Canada in the 1980s, a slightly higher proportion than Canada's 65% or so (Figure 11.1). This proportion ranges from a low of about 61% in Newfoundland to a high of 72.5% in Prince Edward Island. Service industries encompass many activities, from cutting hair to selling real estate, retailing and wholesaling, transporting goods and people, and tending to their health.

Gradually, since the Second World War, services have gradually and substantially supplanted goods production throughout North America. They have been a primary source of new jobs. Since 1977 in Atlantic Canada, four out of every five new jobs have been in services. The sector has been the principal source of employment for females. Services concentrate in towns and cities. In the Halifax metro area, almost 90% of all employment is in services, with similar degrees of concentration in other

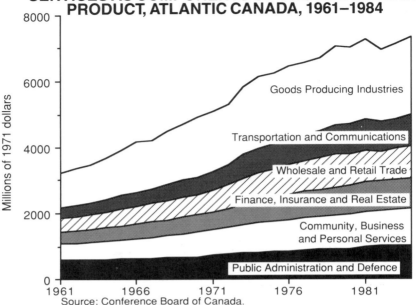

FIGURE 11.1: GROSS DOMESTIC PRODUCT, AND SERVICES AS COMPONENTS OF GROSS DOMESTIC PRODUCT, ATLANTIC CANADA, 1961–1984

Goods Producing Industries

Transportation and Communications

Wholesale and Retail Trade

Finance, Insurance and Real Estate

Community, Business and Personal Services

Public Administration and Defence

Millions of 1971 dollars

Source: Conference Board of Canada.

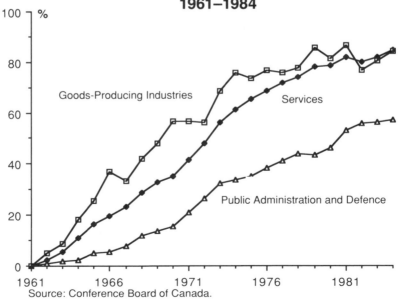

FIGURE 11.2: CUMULATIVE PERCENTAGE CHANGE IN OUTPUT OF SERVICE INDUSTRIES, GOODS PRODUCING INDUSTRIES, AND PUBLIC ADMINISTRATION AND DEFENCE, ATLANTIC CANADA, 1961–1984

Goods-Producing Industries

Services

Public Administration and Defence

Source: Conference Board of Canada.

big regional centres. Some of this employment (for example, professional occupations) requires highly skilled and qualified manpower with incomes to match. At the opposite end of the spectrum are the most menial of tasks requiring few skills, and low wages; they offer workers little opportunity for career advancement, and make them vulnerable to exploitation by employers, and to economic recession.

Development of Services

One theory of the development of services sees them as direct results of growth in goods production. As a sophisticated interdependence between primary production and secondary manufacturing develops, functions previously conducted within a firm will be contracted out to firms that specialise in supplying that service. Also, as government regulation expands, services such as accounting and auditing need to be provided by qualified firms.

This theory should see services expanding and contracting more or less in line with output of goods. In fact, fluctuations in service provision over time have been more moderate than for goods production (Figure 11.2). Certainly, annual variation in goods production in Atlantic Canada has been wider than service provision, indicating that services may provide some stability of employment and income during cyclical ups and downs. The presence of a substantial and stable government sector helps provide this cushion, and other services (trade, transportation, and communications, for example) have wider swings as they depend more on goods production.

Some services are now regarded as independent generators of economic progress, especially in the fields of finance, insurance and professional activities. The ability to derive more benefits from such services, of course, relies eventually on expanding beyond local or regional markets; Atlantic Canada has probably benefited less from such service growth than have big central provinces.

Types of Service Industries

There are five generally-accepted categories of services:

- Transportation and communications
- Finance, insurance and real estate
- Wholesale and retail trade
- Community, business, and personal services
- Public administration and defence

TABLE 11.1: VALUE OF OUTPUT FROM THE SERVICE SECTOR, ATLANTIC CANADA SELECTED YEARS 1961 TO 1986

	1961	1965	1970	1975	1980	1985
Transportation and communications:						
(1) $ million (1971)	326	420	528	780	910	1000
(2) % of all services	14.9	16.4	17.0	18.9	19.3	17.7
Finance, insurance and real estate:						
(1) $ million (1971)	373	434	523	698	873	955
(2) % of all services	17.1	20.1	16.9	17.0	18.5	16.9
Wholesale and retail trade:						
(1) $ million (1971)	409	516	623	882	970	1117
(2) % of all services	18.7	20.1	20.1	21.4	20.6	19.8
Community, business and personal services:						
(1) $ million (1971)	487	574	741	930	1,031	1,505
(2) % of all services	22.3	22.4	23.9	22.6	21.9	26.7
Public administration and defence:						
(1) $ million (1971)	588	619	684	829	924	1057
(2) % of all services	26.9	24.2	22.1	20.1	19.6	18.7
All services:						
(1) $ million (1971)	2,183	2,563	3,099	4,119	4,708	5,636
All services as % of gdp	64.8	65.4	62.9	65.8	67.1	68.7

Source: Conference Board of Canada

The value of output of all services in Atlantic Canada went up by an annual average rate of 4% in real terms between 1961 and 1985 (Table 11.1).

Transportation and communication, which include the various modes of transportation, storage and distribution, and communications industries such as radio, television, and telephones, have increased their share of the value of all services from about 15% to almost 18% since 1961; this reflects increases in both level and types of services available. Means of communication have developed considerably since the early 1960s, particularly as technological advances have provided access to commercially available services, even in the most remote parts of the region. (See

Chapter 13 for more details on the transportation and communications industry.)

Finance, insurance and real estate accounted for 17% of the value of all services in 1985, the same as in 1961 although there has been variation over the years. It is especially important in Newfoundland and Nova Scotia and in the region's bigger urban centres; cities like Halifax, in particular, have concentrations of regional offices.

Wholesale and retail trades have more or less maintained a one-fifth share of all services over the years. Consumer spending has long been an important part of economic progress in Atlantic Canada, and the movement of goods through warehouses and shops reflects this importance. Actual retail sales in the region increased at an average annual rate of almost 11% between 1971 and 1985 in real terms.

Within the retail sector small, usually family-owned stores are giving way to regional or national chains. Trade through chain outlets in Atlantic Canada increased as a proportion of total trade from 1971 to 1986, from 35% to 40%; this was at the expense of trade through independent outlets. The number of department stores in the region went up from 42 in 1971 to 79 in 1984. There has been an increase in the number of shopping malls. In 1970, there were 19 shopping centres in the Atlantic provinces, including eight each in Nova Scotia and New Brunswick; three years later there were 36, and in 1986 there were 125 of over 50,000 square feet each. The number of franchise outlets is also increasing.

Community, business and personal services, which include a wide range of educational, medical, legal, social, religious, recreational, professional, accommodation, food and many other services, have become the biggest single sector in the Atlantic economy. In 1985, the sector accounted for 18.3% of regional gross domestic product compared with, for example, 11.5% for manufacturing. The total sector is diverse, ranging from some of the most highly-paid professional services to lower-paid everyday jobs.

Community, business and personal services perhaps best illustrate the dynamism and growth of a modern economy. New types of services rapidly emerge; these usually require less in the way of high investment (save setting up an office) to test markets. For example, there were virtually no computer services in Atlantic Canada in 1971, but there are many of them in the late 1980s. Numbers of movie theatres and shoe-repair services, conversely, have declined over the years. This sector perhaps offers the best and easiest opportunities for individuals to put ideas into commercial practice.

TABLE 11.2: SELECTED HEALTH AND EDUCATION OCCUPATION STATISTICS, ATLANTIC PROVINCES, 1974 AND 1984

	Newfoundland and Labrador 1974	1984	Prince Edward Island 1974	1984	Nova Scotia 1974	1984	New Brunswick 1974	1984
Civilian doctors	660	981	114	158	1,321	1,720	726	*937*
Dentists	63	135	41	44	236	352	137	*211*
Veterinarians	13	24	21	34	65	115	56	*89*
Licensed Nurses	3,013	5,142	951	1,181	5,921	9,047	6,429	*7,676*
Pharmacists	176	395	35	53	352	631	238	*398*
Optometrists	16	35	6	8	37	55	42	*77*
University teachers	747	892	117	*118*	*1471*	*1902*	*1011*	*1135*
School teachers	7,409	8,216	1,391	1,300	10,811	10,563	7,901	*7475*

Source: Health and Welfare Canada, *Canada Health Manpower Inventory 1984;* Statistics Canada Catalogue 81-229.

TABLE 11.3: GOVERNMENT EMPLOYMENT AND PAYROLLS, ATLANTIC PROVINCES AND CANADA, 1985 (1)

	Federal	Provincial [1]	Municipal [2]	All Governments
Newfoundland and Labrador [3]:				
Employment	7,727	21,987	2,404	32,118
Payroll ($ million)	*4.7*	*13.2*	*1.4*	*19.3*
Prince Edward Island:				
Employment	3,397	4,404	2,643	10,444
As % of all employed	7.2	9.4	5.6	22.2
Payroll ($ million)	98.0	92.3	56.1	246.1
Nova Scotia:				
Employment	33,371	21,685	28,041	83,097
As % of all employed	10.0	6.5	8.4	24.8
Payroll ($ million)	909.1	495.0	670.8	2,074.8
New Brunswick[3]				
Employment	13,005	32,600	3,937	49,452
As % of all employed	5.1	12.7	1.6	19.3
Payroll ($ million)	361.8	779.3	99.4	1,240.4
Canada:				
Employment	375,516	473,772	818,185	1,667,473
As % of all employed	3.3	4.1	7.2	14.6
Payroll ($ million)	17,531.8	12,224.1	20,754.9	50,510.8

Notes: 1. Including military personnel.
2. Including school boards.
3. Large areas of Newfoundland and New Brunswick are not organised into municipal units, so school boards are provincially run.

Sources: Statistics Canada Catalogues 71-001, 72-004, 72-007, 72-009

Atlantic Canada Today

Expansion of health and education services reflects Atlantic Canada's growth as a sophisticated, twentieth-century society. Employment data illustrate this expansion, with strong increases in all four provinces since 1974 (Table 11.2). A wider range of specialised services has become available, and there has been associated growth of technical and research support.

Public administration and defence are more important to the Atlantic economy than to anywhere else in Canada. In part, this is because four small provinces each maintains separate government structures, as well as having regional and/or provincial offices of federal departments. There is, as well, a substantial military presence on the East Coast, with Halifax being the headquarters of Canada's Maritime Command.

Public administration and defence have occupied a gradually declining share of gross domestic product, especially as government restraint has taken hold in the 1980s. In Atlantic Canada, however, it remains the most important single sector after community, business and personal services. A measure of its importance comes from employment and payroll data (Table 11.3). There were 175,000 government jobs in the region in 1985, with a total payroll of more than $430 million.

Summary

The service sector has added substantial benefits to the region's economy, and will continue to do so. It has been a prime source of new jobs, and has offered many small entrepreneurs a relatively easy way to set up their own businesses. It includes advanced research capability, ranging from agricultural stations to cold water research. Higher education and health services have developed, which also involve aspects of advanced research. This not only offers Atlantic Canadians enviable access to educational opportunities and health care, but also provides a means for further research endeavours which attract highly paid personnel.

There are some difficulties with increasing dependence on service industries. There is a higher incidence of unskilled, low-income work, much of it part-time. There is less investment in services than is usually associated with goods production. Expansion into export markets has been limited. And there are perennial claims that productivity within the sector has been, and will remain, low.

Emphasis on service industries, however, is particularly appropriate in the late twentieth century. The so-called "information revolution" provides new opportunities. Many new service industries are not as location-specific as traditional ones, which are bound by such factors as considerations of material inputs, established reserves of skills, and transportation networks. In this kind of environment, parts of the world such as Atlantic Canada can benefit greatly by possessing a world-class telecommunications network as the prime means of reaching their markets.

Further Reading

Task Force on Trade in Services, *Background Report.* Ottawa, 1982

CHAPTER 12

Tourism: The Export That Doesn't Go Anywhere

Tourism is an odd industry. It does not have well-defined edges, but spreads over many other industries such as hotel and food services, transportation, arts and crafts, and so on. It may also be considered an export in that it brings in visitors who then spend money and leave. The things which bring them here, however (scenery, lobster suppers, theatre, sandy beaches), don't leave with them. The only things they take home are photographs, purchased souvenirs, perhaps a sunburn, and memories. Tourism based on scenic attractions, is frequently associated with areas of relative economic disadvantage; rugged, natural beauty is often in remote areas that are relatively undeveloped.

The scope of the industry has broadened. Once considered a "vacation" industry, tourism now encompasses business travel, conventions, major sporting events, visits by prominent people, and festivals. The widest definition is as a "hospitality" industry, which includes anyone, regardless of place of residence, who steps out for an evening's dinner, visits a local lounge, bar, or place of entertainment. The linkages between tourism and retail trades are indeed strong.

This means that data used to measure the economic impact of tourism usually crop up as measures of performance in other sectors, especially services. This makes analysis of tourism in isolation rather hazy. One thing is clear: the industry is, has been for several decades, and will be for the foreseeable future, one of quite spectacular growth in the industrialised world. This is closely linked to levels of wealth, leisure time, disposable incomes, and personal mobility.

Some General Characteristics

Direct tourist spending on domestic travel in Canada in 1984 was $16 or $17 billion, some $1.3 billion of which was in Atlantic Canada. The main components of this spending were transportation (both private and public), food and beverages, accommodation, and recreation and entertainment (Figure 12.1). Trends of visitation and spending have varied. There was a period of rapid growth during the 1960s as the number of visitors from outside the region (especially Americans) increased. This increase slowed during the 1970s when inflation was high. Trends since the mid-1970s have more or less been static.

Travel within Atlantic Canada is an important component of tourism. Most visitors to Nova Scotia in recent years have been from adjacent provinces with significant numbers also from Ontario (as much as 30%) and the United States (up to 55%).[1] Distribution in New Brunswick is different; most auto visitation is from Quebec or Ontario (about 50%) followed by the other Maritime provinces (20%) and New England (10% or 15%). Many of New Brunswick's tourists may be on their way to other parts of Atlantic Canada.

Between 60% and 65% of Prince Edward Island's visitors come from adjacent provinces, with most arriving by private vehicle. There are important markets also in Ontario, Quebec and New England. Between 60% and 70% of Newfoundland's visitors arrive by air, mainly from other Canadian provinces. A good proportion of Newfoundland's tourism is either business-related or the so-called VFR (visiting friends or relations) trade.

Tourist travel within provinces is very important to the region. Some 86% of Newfoundland's Canadian tourists in 1984 lived in the province. While there was also a high proportion of intra-provincial travel for Nova Scotia (71%) and New Brunswick (66%), Prince Edward Island, with only 14%, had the bulk of its visitors from other provinces. In an average tourist year, the Island can expect to entertain numbers of visitors amounting to four or five times its resident population.

Although there have been attempts to diversify the range of tourist attractions in Atlantic Canada, the region still relies on a fairly traditional family-style market based on outdoor activities and scenery. Weather

FIGURE 12.1: PROPORTIONAL DISPOSITION OF TOURIST SPENDING, ATLANTIC PROVINCES & CANADA, 1984*

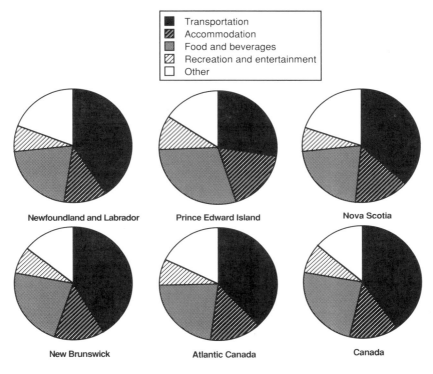

* Note: These proportions are based on tourist spending on domestic travel only.
Source: Statistics Canada Catalogue 87-504

plays an important part in the success of an individual season, since beaches and scenery remain important attractions. Some diversity has been achieved by the addition of festivals and convention centres, and some stability, by the promotion of special themes (for example, parades of sailing ships), "come home" seasons, notable provincial anniversaries, or royal visits.

All four provinces must overcome some difficulties. Both Prince Edward Island and Newfoundland are islands requiring vehicle access by ferry. Newfoundland, as well, is rather remote. New Brunswick suffers from "being on the way there" rather than a destination in its own right. The Maritimes, where there is a high degree of reliance on "impulse" visitation from adjacent provinces, suffers in spells of bad weather, especially if they occur on weekends.

TABLE 12.1: GOVERNMENT REVENUES FROM TOURISM, ATLANTIC PROVINCES, 1984

	Federal	Provincial/Municipal
	– millions of dollars –	
Newfoundland and Labrador	59	35
Prince Edward Island	24	13
Nova Scotia	124	62
New Brunswick	80	44

Source: Canadian Government Office of Tourism

Tourism provides between 10,000 and 15,000 direct jobs during peak periods. These extra jobs are particularly important in Prince Edward Island and Newfoundland (as much as 15% and 8% of all jobs respectively). Governments benefit from taxes on such retail items, gasoline, and alcoholic beverages bought by tourists (Table 12.1).

The Market: An Analysis of Tourist Demand

Economic and demographic factors affect tourism. Increases in the price of oil in the 1970s, for example, began a change in travel patterns that ate into touring by car, a large component of Atlantic tourism. Higher prices in the region, caused in part by higher taxes and offset only to a degree by devaluation of the Canadian dollar, have also discouraged and surprised some American tourists. While higher gasoline prices deter long-distance visitors, they also keep local residents closer to home.

Demographic trends have seen population growth at lower rates in the 1970s and 1980s, and a population which is getting generally older. Greater numbers of older people, often quite affluent, may increase the demand for air travel or organised bus tours. Changes in family structures (fewer children, for example, or waiting longer to have children, or more single-parent families) may result in smaller family parties, which also spend less. However, higher family incomes, as more wives and mothers have gone out to work, make a wider range of vacations affordable. Tourism has become increasingly global, which means that the Atlantic industry must compete intensively with many exotic destinations. (Periodic surges of political instability or terrorism, however, discourage people from going to a given part of the world and may persuade them to stay with something they know is safe.) Given a greatly increased array of opportunities open to them, tourists are becoming more discerning. They pay closer attention to quality of infrastructure and variety of attractions, and carefully weigh strengths and weaknesses of a given area. As tourists become more affluent and cosmopolitan, Atlantic operators must consider ways to compete effectively.

TABLE 12.2: UNITS OF TRAVELLER ACCOMMODATION, ATLANTIC PROVINCES, 1980–1984

	Newfoundland and Labrador	Prince Edward Island	Nova Scotia	New Brunswick	Atlantic Canada
Rooms:					
1980	3,558	2,417	8,590	7,502	22,067
1981	3,639	2,089	8,299	7,470	21,443
1982	3,654	2,167	8,365	7,440	21,626
1983	3,635	2,112	8,376	7,205	21,328
1984	3,627	2,032	8,540	7,135	21,334
Cabins:					
1980	353	852	1,049	691	2,945
1981	369	879	953	681	2,882
1982	427	873	907	658	2,865
1983	458	896	929	654	2,937
1984	428	933	882	544	2,787
Tent/trailer spaces:					
1980	4,143	6,779	13,264	11,406	35,592
1981	4,096	6,471	13,099	11,258	34,874
1982	4,013	6,497	11,670	11,312	33,492
1983	3,874	6,244	11,837	10,626	32,581
1984	4,095	6,363	11,831	11,521	33,810

Source: Statistics Canada Catalogue 62-204

Infrastructure: An Analysis of Supply

Atlantic Canada abounds in the natural and physical attractions that lure tourists. Some of these attractions are showcased in provincial or national parks, historic places, or museums. Often they are supplemented by cultural events that emphasise an area's heritage and history. Atlantic Canadians themselves are considered to be a major attraction because of their friendliness and openness. To complete the tourism package, there is a complex infrastructure of accommodations, eating places, transportation links, and information services.

Numbers of accommodation units (rooms, cabins, or tent/trailer spaces) have declined slightly since 1980. Roofed accommodation is concentrated more in bigger centres, where there are more attractions and higher occupancy rates (Table 12.2). As with many other industries in Atlantic Canada, seasonality is a problem and results in over-capacity. Seasonality of employment also restricts the acquisition of skills, an important consideration in attempts to develop a sophisticated industry.

The challenge presented by seasonality, is to extend the season beyond the traditional two or three months of summer. Convention centres and new hotels now attract national and international meetings and sports events. "Shoulder season" attractions (such as the fall leaves) are aimed at bus tours, usually of older people who prefer to avoid the heat and crowds of summer. Specialised attractions, usually sold as package tours, can bring in affluent tourists who are willing to spend more for what they regard as a unique experience; angling for tuna off Prince Edward Island brings in fishermen from all over the world, as does salmon fishing throughout the region.

Governments in the region have a great interest in the success of tourism and maintain departments, or parts of departments, with responsibilities for information dissemination, regulation of certain types of accommodation such as camping grounds, and promotion. Total spending by departments on main non-administrative items in the region amounted to $40 million, or about 23% of all such spending in Canada. There are, as well, federal-provincial sub-agreements to address tourist development; the current ones to run to 1989 and contain $76 million in the four provinces.

Summary

Atlantic Canada has much to offer tourists. Strengths include geographic diversity, friendly and approachable residents, effective information and booking services, a wide variety of accommodation and food outlets, and specialised infrastructure such as convention centres.

The industry is, however, hindered by a number of weaknesses: a high degree of seasonality, which deters capital formation in infrastructure, and affects skill-development in related employment; some transportation difficulties where configuration of land and water are allied to dispersion of attractions; high prices for certain key items, boosted by provincial taxes; and some dissipation of promotional effort by individual provinces, who tend to emphasise Atlantic attractions in isolation rather than contributing to a well-rounded and diverse whole.

The tourist industry around the world changes rapidly, as do markets and types of demand. To compete effectively requires slick promotion, more diversity of attractions, less emphasis on seasons, and a keen awareness of emerging demographic and economic trends.

Footnotes:

1. Data on tourism, which overlaps with so many other sectors, are difficult to compile. Many are collected by surveys which, for example, cover only the main tourist season and concentrate only on out-of-province visitation by counting licence plates. As such, they cover only the "export" component of tourism.

Further Reading

Minister of State (Tourism), *Tourism Tomorrow: Towards a Canadian Tourism Strategy.* Ottawa, 1985.

Statistics Canada, *Tourism and Recreation Statistical Digest.* Ottawa, 1986.

CHAPTER 13

Transportation and Communication: Moving People, Goods, and Information

An ungainly configuration of land and water means special problems in moving around Atlantic Canada. A system of highways, railways, ferries, airlines, and coastal shipping must often take circuitous routes to reach a destination. A dispersed and sometimes sparse settlement pattern adds to the difficulties. Many communities remain isolated, particularly in Newfoundland and Labrador.

As the region's economy has grown, so have the means to move people and things. As seen in Chapter 11, transportation and communications as an industry accounts for about 18% of gross domestic product in Atlantic Canada. Physical movement has been complemented by development of a very sophisticated telecommunications network.

Movement of People

People move in Atlantic Canada by private auto, train, bus, ferry, and aeroplane. The car has come to dominate many aspects of personal travel, although public transport tends to increase over longer distances.

TABLE 13.1: PASSENGER CAR REGISTRATION, ATLANTIC PROVINCES AND CANADA 1960 AND 1985

	1960	1985	Annual average change 1960–1985
			– percent –
Newfoundland and Labrador	45,586	168,416	5.4
Prince Edward Island	19,170	54,533	4.3
Nova Scotia	140,151	366,172	3.9
New Brunswick	106,167	278,106	3.9
Atlantic Canada	311,074	867,227	4.2
Canada	4,104,415	11,118,471	4.1

Source: Statistics Canada Catalogue 53-219

Private Cars. Growth in numbers of cars on Atlantic highways has been accompanied by great improvements to the highways themselves. In 1949, there were about 55,200 km of road in the region, of which less than 150 km had some kind of pavement; the majority were gravel or earth. In the late 1980s, the only remaining concentration of earth roads serves rural areas of Prince Edward Island, and of about 70,000 km of roads and streets about half is paved. This includes a series of all-weather roads based on the Trans-Canada Highway. Atlantic Canadians registered 311,074 cars in 1960, or 164 per 1,000 people; by 1985 there were 867,227 cars registered, or 376 per 1,000 people (Table 13.1). Population between the two years went up by about 21%, car ownership by 178%.

While the amount of freight traffic on the highways is fairly predictable year-round, the number of cars fluctuates with the time of day, and in the case of popular tourist areas, season of the year. The cost of gasoline also affects car travel, although higher prices since the mid-1970s has not necessarily seen fewer cars on the highways, rather many more smaller ones.

Rail and Bus. Canada's railway system essentially exists for movement of freight rather than people, but train travel is still quite substantial. Any reductions have been caused by more car travel and improved air service. Canadian National in 1960 reported a national ridership of more than 11 million passengers over a total of almost 18 billion passenger-kilometres. In the 1980s, these numbers are about 6 million passengers over about 2.5 billion passenger-kilometres. Passenger service by rail remains only in Nova Scotia and New Brunswick. Travel by bus is still

FIGURE 13.1: PASSENGERS AND PRIVATE CARS ON MARINE ATLANTIC'S FIVE PRINCIPAL SERVICES, 1980–1986

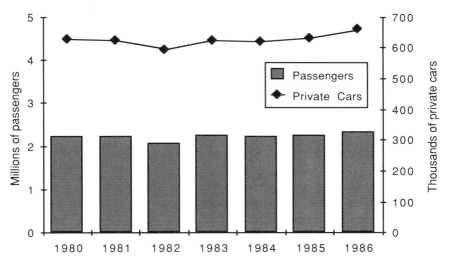

Note: The five services are, in descending order of ridership, between Cape Tormentine, New Brunswick, and Borden, Prince Edward Island; North Sydney, Nova Scotia, and Saint John, New Brunswick; Yarmouth, Nova Scotia, and Bar Harbour, Maine; and North Sydney, Nova Scotia, and Argentia, Newfoundland. Other important ferry services (not run by Marine Atlantic) link Caribou, Nova Scotia and Wood Islands, Prince Edward Island; and Yarmouth, Nova Scotia, and Portland, Maine.

Source: Marine Atlantic.

important within major urban centres but has declined between towns and cities. Most inter-urban travel has become the domain of cars and aeroplanes.

Ferries. Surface transportation in Atlantic Canada moves from land to sea by means of a fleet of ferries ranging in size from a cross-river barge to ocean-going vessels capable of ice-breaking. Both the region's island provinces have constitutional guarantees of year-round ferry connections to the mainland, and the ferries are vital in the movement of both people and commodities. These ferry services receive federal subsidies.

More than 2.3 million passengers rode on Marine Atlantic's five principal services in 1986 (Figure 13.1). About 75% of these were on a single service, between Cape Tormentine, New Brunswick, and Borden, Prince Edward Island. Many, less frequently travelled services are nonetheless important in maintaining links with coastal communities in Newfoundland and Labrador.

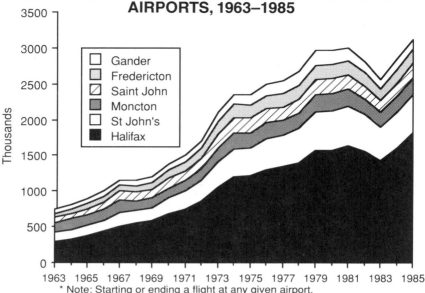

FIGURE 13.2: PASSENGERS ENPLANING AND DEPLANING* AT ATLANTIC CANADA'S SIX BUSIEST AIRPORTS, 1963–1985

Legend:
- Gander
- Fredericton
- Saint John
- Moncton
- St John's
- Halifax

* Note: Starting or ending a flight at any given airport.
Source: Statistics CanadaCatalogues 51-005 and 51-203.

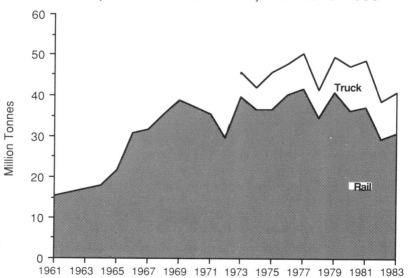

FIGURE 13.3: FREIGHT TRANSPORTED BY RAIL AND ROAD, ATLANTIC CANADA, 1961/1973–1983

Note: Rail freight is loadings. Road freight is in "for-hire" trucks.
No truck figures before 1973.
Source: Statistics Canada Catalogues 52-205 and 53-224.

Air. Air travel in Atlantic Canada has grown markedly since the early 1960s. Two Class I carriers (Air Canada and Canadian Airlines International) provide direct flights to other parts of Canada, the United States, and Europe. Other carriers provide service between centres within Atlantic Canada.

The number of passengers at the region's six busiest airports went up by a factor of about four between 1963 and the early 1980s (Figure 13.2). Air travel has responded quite closely to business conditions, with declines or plateaux in the mid-1970s and the early 1980s substantially explained by recession. Halifax has the region's busiest airport, and has recorded the most solid and rapid increase in numbers of passengers handled.

Movement of Commodities

Road and Rail. Most of Atlantic Canada's products make at least part of their journey to market by truck or train. A few commodities account for most of the tonnage, a fact that influences the stability of freight haulage. Rail freight is dominated by minerals, especially iron ore in Labrador, coal and gypsum in Nova Scotia, and zinc and potash in New Brunswick. Shipment by road is relatively more important for forest products, especially getting pulpwood to mills.

The domination of iron ore shows up in Figure 13.3. When mines in Labrador began operations in the early 1960s, total tonnage shipped by rail increased from a little over 15 million tonnes in 1961 to almost 40 million tonnes in 1969. Subsequent ups and downs reflect recessions in the early 1970s, the mid-1970s, and the early 1980s. A big dip in 1978 was due to a strike at the mines.

Atlantic Canada has a skeletal network of railways. Main lines still run to other parts of Canada, chiefly from important ports such as Halifax and Saint John, but elsewhere spurs remain. These allow shipments of gypsum from Windsor to Halifax, potash from Sussex to Saint John, zinc ores from mines in interior northern New Brunswick to Belledune, and coal in industrial Cape Breton. There are difficulties in providing rail service to Prince Edward Island and Newfoundland because of sea crossings. In Newfoundland, as well, the railway is a narrower-than-standard gauge, necessitating trans-shipment between railcars, or equipment adjustment when goods enter or leave the province by rail.

Freight that travels by rail is usually high bulk and unmanufactured. Most general freight traffic has been taken over by trucks, a trend once again complemented by improvement in the region's road system. There was a fourfold increase in numbers of trucks operating between 1960 and 1984 in Atlantic Canada. Part of this increase involved products shipped from Prince Edward Island and Newfoundland; commercial crossings from Port aux Basques to North Sydney went up from 2,000 in 1966 to 47,500 in 1986. Completion of Newfoundland's portion of the Trans-Canada Highway during this period greatly assisted this trend.

Truck freight in 1973 (that carried on "for-hire" trucks only) was less than 6 million tonnes; it was about 10 million tonnes in the early 1980s (Figure 13.3). Total volumes carried correspond quite closely with output of manufacturing industries and overall economic conditions, and about 20% of all loads originate in the construction sector. The flexibility of truck haulage is an important advantage when products are perishable, or must be delivered from door to door.

Movement of many commodities by rail or truck both within Atlantic Canada and to destinations west of Lévis, Quebec, is subsidised by federal authorities under the Maritime Freight Rates Act and the closely related Atlantic Region Freight Assistance Act. The amount of this subsidy in the late 1980s is $60 to $70 million, and it has become such an important part of production and shipping that suggestions of reducing or removing it have met fervent opposition.

Water Transport. Atlantic ports are well placed to ship both to Europe and eastern North America. Much of the history of the region has involved trade by sea and strong maritime traditions. The late twentieth century sees containers moving through Halifax and Saint John, being carried in unit trains to and from central Canada, and being trucked to and from plants within the region.

Halifax and Saint John have the region's best port infrastructures, with grain elevators at Halifax, and specialised mineral-loading facilities and container terminals at both ports. Both have oil refineries that depend on imports of crude oil from overseas, and that also ship refined products to markets by water. Tonnages shipped have increased quite strongly over the years, once again allowing for cyclical movements in the larger economy (Figure 13.4).

The rapid spread of container shipping has ramifications for Atlantic business. Container ships run on fixed routes according to fixed schedules. Originally, these were along heavily travelled commercial routes such as the north Atlantic between eastern North America and western Europe. Later developments have seen the rise of round-the-world services in both eastern and western directions, and usually with bigger ships. (Some ships, indeed have become so big that they cannot

FIGURE 13.4: CARGOES SHIPPED THROUGH THE PORTS OF HALIFAX AND SAINT JOHN, 1960, 1965, 1970, 1975, and 1980–1986

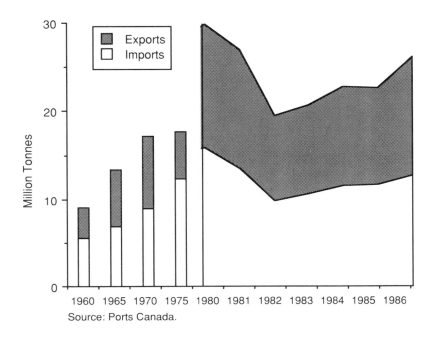

Source: Ports Canada.

traverse the Panama Canal, necessitating "land-bridging" across North America as part of a round-the-world service.) Regular stops by such a service at Atlantic ports give Atlantic products access to a wider range of markets than ever before, and reduce costs of shipping to within the budget of many smaller companies; it is easier to fill a container than it is to fill an entire ship.

Specific resources are shipped from other ports in the region. Pulp and paper products are shipped from many smaller ports such as Stephenville in Newfoundland; Liverpool, Port Hawkesbury and Pictou in Nova Scotia; and Bathurst and the Miramichi ports in New Brunswick. There are seasonal flurries of activity at ports in both Prince Edward Island and New Brunswick to accommodate shipments of potatoes. Metal ores and coal move through ports in New Brunswick and Nova Scotia, as well as pulpwood going to export markets.

Air Freight. Some 25 million kg of products were shipped by air in 1983, a big increase from 7.5 million kg in 1963. Most of this growth has gone through airports at Halifax and St John's, and must be closely related to offshore exploration. Urgency, value of product, and perishability are important considerations when choosing this relatively expensive mode of shipping. It is an area that has been growing quite rapidly, especially as a means of marketing fresh fish all over the world.

Transportation: Tool of Development, Constitutional Right, or Commercial Enterprise?

The nature of Canada necessitates an enhanced role for transportation. Most of the 25 million inhabitants live in a strip of land about 150 km wide and 6,400 km long. These settlement difficulties are aggravated in Atlantic Canada for reasons already noted.

Transportation issues, therefore, have had a fervency and stridency of their own. Transportation policies have been de facto industrial programs, and erosion of these programs has occasionally dealt severe blows to the Atlantic economy. Federal transport subsidies affecting Atlantic Canada have grown over the years, mainly as governments and businesses have kept reminding other Canadians of their constitutional obligations. Basically, these state that no part of Canada should be at a competitive disadvantage because of the costs of transporting products to market.

The story behind the beginnings of the Maritime Freight Rates Act (MFRA) and Atlantic Region Freight Assistance Act (ARFAA) has been mentioned several times already in this book. MFRA emerged from the recommendations of the Duncan Royal Commission in 1927, a Commission itself set up to examine the claims of the Maritime Rights Movement. ARFAA supplemented MFRA in 1969. The two acts are designed to restore a degree of competitiveness for regional producers both within Atlantic Canada and in the important central markets of Ontario and Quebec. Both have been threatened, examined, reduced, and studied over the years. One study, commissioned in 1983, estimated that removal of MFRA/ARFAA would result in the loss of 5,400 jobs, and reduce income to businesses by $157 million.

The constitutional/developmental/commercial aspects of transportation are not always separable. In some respects, such as building and maintaining infrastructure, there is a clear public responsibility to be financed by taxes. But a large grey area surrounds subsidies. It is probable, for example, that subsidies under MFRA/ARFAA have been capitalised into the assets of companies that use them; reduction or removal of the subsidies would impose a cost that may threaten the survival of firms, or cause them to relocate outside Atlantic Canada.

TABLE 13.2: AMOUNTS OF SELECTED TRANSPORTATION SUBSIDIES IN ATLANTIC CANADA 1983/84

Subsidy	Amount
	– $ million –
Maritime Freight Rates Act / Atlantic Region Freight Assistance Act	62
Marine Atlantic	174
Feed Freight Assistance Act[1]	6
At-and-East[2]	35

Notes: 1) The bulk of this subsidy (totalling $15.9 million in 1983/84) covers feed grain shipments from Ontario or the Prairie provinces to Quebec ($3.7 million) and British Columbia ($5.8 million).
2) This assists shipments of grain and flour to point of export in East Coast ports including Saint John and Halifax.

Sources: Canadian Transportation Commission; Marine Atlantic; Livestock Feed Board of Canada

In such terms, subsidies decrease economic efficiency and inhibit the movement of resources to their best end uses. There have been claims, as well, that MFRA/ARFAA have deterred industrial development in Prince Edward Island and Newfoundland. Both island markets can just as easily be supplied from plants in Nova Scotia or New Brunswick, which are aided by transportation assistance. Subsidising the movement of raw material inputs to plants outside the region may have inhibited more local manufacture of these resources. Ferry subsidies are industrial assistance to Prince Edward Island, Newfoundland, and western Nova Scotia; feed grain subsidies assist many livestock farmers in the region; and the 'At and East' grain and flour subsidies support jobs in the docks in Halifax and Saint John. (An indication of the amount of principal subsidies is in Table 13.2.)

Consideration of transportation issues in Atlantic Canada intensified in the mid-1980s as deregulation of many parts of the industry was introduced. Supporters of deregulation in the United States point to more efficient trucking industries, or wider availability of reasonably priced air travel as sure signs of an idea whose time has come. These have not been achieved painlessly, however, and it is doubtful whether the Canadian situation provides a close parallel to the American. American markets are bigger and more concentrated, and economies of scale are easier to achieve. By the same token, deregulation could benefit southern Ontario and Quebec more than Atlantic Canada.

TABLE 13.3: NEWSPAPER STATISTICS, ATLANTIC PROVINCES, 1985

	Dailies[1]		Weeklies[1]	
	Number	Circulation	Number	Circulation
Newfoundland and Labrador	2	103,500	17	102,013
Prince Edward Island	2	34,382	4	30,839
Nova Scotia	6	205,870	36	172,766
New Brunswick	4	208,582	22	239,653
Atlantic Canada	14	552,334	79	545,271

Note (1) Dailies include three with both morning and evening editions. There is one French-language daily in New Brunswick. The weeklies include one French-language in each of Newfoundland, Prince Edward Island and Nova Scotia; and four French-language and two bilingual in New Brunswick.

Source: Audit Bureau of Circulation

Communications

Communications industries deal more with movement of information and intelligence than goods and people. The means of communicating between people have changed with bewildering speed in the twentieth century, a rate of change that continues. Word processors have effectively made authors into typesetters; this book in its final stages was written on a personal computer, the text transferred to diskettes, and typeset automatically from those diskettes. Faster and more accurate data and information management and manipulation has been made possible by the silicon chip and a sophisticated telephone system. Even the remotest homes can receive many television stations by means of a satellite receiving dish.

Newspapers. Journalism has an honourable tradition in Atlantic Canada. Weekly and daily newspapers in the region had a combined circulation of more than one million copies in 1985 (Table 13.3). There is a full array of community, trade and specialist publications based in the region, and access to periodicals from other parts of Canada and around the world.

Radio and Television. The majority of North Americans, for better or worse, garner most of their everyday information from radio and, especially, television. Both media have moulded the twentieth century, bringing sounds and sights from around the world to individual homes. The ability of television in particular to influence thought is considerable, as any advertiser can attest. Appearance and style on television can also make or break political careers. There are about 725,000 television sets

TABLE 13.4: RADIO AND TELEVISION STATISTICS, ATLANTIC PROVINCES AND CANADA, 1972 AND 1984

	Newfoundland and Labrador	Prince Edward Island	Nova Scotia	New Brunswick	Canada
Radio Stations:					
1972	18	2	17	15	338
1984	78	8	60	61	1,289
Television Stations:					
1972	34	1	13	9	401
1984	128	7	54	35	1,194
Cable Television Companies:					
1972	1	—	5	8	344
1984	28	20	40	37	811
Cable Television Subscribers:					
1972	290	—	10,171	11,292	1,689,335
1984	59,000	16,000	148,000	106,000	5,319,000

Source: *Canadian Almanac*

in households in Atlantic Canada in the late 1980s, and 99% of all households have at least one set. Some 45% of households, indeed, have two or more sets. There are about 320 sets for every 1,000 people.

Television ownership is directly related to receiving a clear signal. It has been easier in this respect to provide service to concentrations of population, and some rural areas in Atlantic Canada still receive inferior signals. The spread of television and radio since the early 1970s has, however, been extremely rapid (Table 13.4). Commercial services have increased in number, and have expanded the range of their transmission; cable companies have made many more channels available (including pay channels) using either microwave networks, or satellite receiving dishes, which have allowed services in many smaller communities away from main microwave systems. The satellite dish itself has become an individual consumer item found with increasing frequency in many yards.

Telecommunications. Atlantic Canada has a long association with telecommunications. Alexander Graham Bell maintained a residence in Baddeck, Nova Scotia; Gugliemo Marconi received his first transatlantic wireless radio telegraph messages at Signal Hill, St John's, Newfoundland, and sent his first from a hill in eastern Cape Breton. Today, telecommunications are integral parts of private and business life, and are

TABLE 13.5: TELEPHONE STATISTICS, ATLANTIC PROVINCES AND CANADA, 1963 AND 1985

	Newfoundland and Labrador	Prince Edward Island	Nova Scotia	New Brunswick	Canada
Number of telephones:					
1963	74,099	23,500	202,874	152,922	6,656,613
1985	196,900	52,816	385,739	317,631	12,480,666
Telephones per 100 people:					
1963	15.2	22.0	26.6	24.9	34.8
1985	33.9	41.3	43.7	44.1	48.9
Percent of telephones on party lines:					
1963	51.7	58.1	33.0	47.1	36.0
1985	3.7	27.2	12.2	12.2	10.3
Phone calls per 1,000 people:					
1963	475	379	518	418	592
1985	3,401	1,951	2,094	1,212	1,361

Source: Statistics Canada Catalogue 56-203

undergoing a revolution of dizzying proportions as part of the information age.

Canadians' love for the telephone is partly due to the distances over which business and personal matters must frequently be discussed. Both use and adoption of telephones has expanded rapidly (Table 13.5). In Newfoundland and Nova Scotia, indeed, people talk more on the phone than anywhere else in Canada.

Few technologies have emerged so rapidly as the telephone. The Atlantic system is as modern as any in the world, with traditional copper cable being steadily replaced by fibre optics. These have a larger capacity to carry signals with freedom from electrical interference. Most messages move throughout the region using microwave networks, with longer distance communications using satellites. Direct dialling now extends around the globe, and telephones are even available in vehicles as they travel.

Some relics remain. Some 27% of telephones in Prince Edward Island (about 12,500) are still on party lines, some 12% in both New Brunswick and Nova Scotia, and 4% in Newfoundland. Mostly, these are in rural areas with dispersed settlement. As older equipment wears out, however, it is replaced by the most modern technologies. Such technologies now

Atlantic Canada Today

allow transmission of audio and visual signals, videotex, and special services for the hard-of-hearing. Access to data banks has become commonplace, complemented by the rise in popularity in homes and businesses of the personal computer.

Summary

Transportation and communications are vital parts of the Atlantic economy. More than many other sectors, change is rapid, and the late twentieth century sees many new influences. Deregulation of many aspects of transportation will bring change, and the increased use of containers will make it easier to ship Atlantic products to many more destinations and markets around the world.

The spread of telecommunications services and technology is especially important. Good information is an integral part of business success. Access to this information is now easier than at any time before, over a wider area, and by many more people. Now that the telephone can put people in touch with markets around the world, this will allow the spread of enterprises run from homes. This locational advantage is a big step in a part of the world not always regarded as being at the centre of things.

Further Reading

Atlantic Provinces Transportation Commission, *Transportation Review and Annual Report*. Moncton, annual.

James F. Hickling Management Consultants Ltd., *The Impact of Freight Transportation Subsidies under the Maritime Freight Rates Act and the Atlantic Region Freight Assistance Act*. Prepared for Transport Canada. Ottawa, 1983.

Lesser, B. and P. Hall, *Telecommunications Services and Regional Development: The Case of Atlantic Canada*. The Institute for Research on Public Policy, Halifax, 1987.

Transport Canada, *Canadian Freight Transportation System Performance & Issues: A Discussion Paper*. Intermodal Freight Branch, Systems Planning Directorate, Strategic Planning Group, Ottawa, 1981.

Transport Canada, *Freedom to Move: A Framework for Transportation Reform*. Honourable D. Mazankowski, Minister of Transport, Ottawa, 1985. Also *Freedom to Move: Change, Choice, Challenge*. Sixth Report of the House of Commons Standing Committee on Transport, P. Nowlan M.P., Chairman, Ottawa, 1985.

Uhm, I. and P. Wesley, *An Examination of the Impact of the 'At and East' Grain and Flour Subsidy Program*. Canadian Transport Commission, Research Branch Working Paper 10-84-10, Ottawa 1984.

CHAPTER 14

Labour Markets: Human Energy and Resourcefulness

Discussion of labour trends embraces business conditions, regional economic structures, demographic developments, individual expectations and aspirations, levels of education, and a host of societal factors. The ultimate aim of any manpower policy is to create jobs for everyone who needs them, to enable them to establish a reasonable standard of living.

Atlantic Canada's success in attaining this objective has been rather spotty. There has been an impressive record of job creation in many sectors, but the numbers of people wanting jobs has usually exceeded the jobs available. Unemployment, sometimes at chronic levels, characterises the region, as do low participation rates, narrow job opportunities, low labour incomes. The migration of Atlantic Canadians to other parts to find work has generally been condemned as eroding the region's capacity to improve its economic lot, but improvements have been too slow in coming to satisfy many of these people.

Like other economic commodities, labour is traded in return for a price, in this case wages. If labour supply at a given time exceeds labour demand, wages should decline; in the opposite situation, wages should increase. However, since we are dealing with people, their sensibilities and their dignity, it is inappropriate to treat labour as a simple commodity.

TABLE 14.1: WORKING AGE POPULATION, LABOUR FORCE, AND PARTICIPATION RATES, ATLANTIC PROVINCES AND CANADA, 1951, 1961, 1971, 1981, AND 1986

	1951	1961	1971	1981	1986
Newfoundland and Labrador:					
Population 15 and over ('000)	220	266	328	396	427
Labour force ('000)	107	114	152	226	226
Participation rate (percent)	48.6	42.9	46.3	51.1	53.0
Prince Edward Island:					
Population 15 and over ('000)	66	67	76	91	96
Labour force ('000)	34	34	44	56	60
Participation rate (percent)	51.6	50.7	57.9	61.6	62.3
Nova Scotia:					
Population 15 and over ('000)	433	481	548	641	671
Labour force ('000)	222	239	292	378	398
Participation rate (percent)	51.2	49.7	53.3	59.0	59.3
New Brunswick:					
Population 15 and over ('000)	332	371	431	516	542
Labour force ('000)	169	180	228	300	312
Participation rate (percent)	51.1	48.5	52.8	58.2	57.5
Canada:					
Population 15 and over ('000)	9,759	12,046	15,189	18,609	19,594
Labour force ('000)	5,299	6,510	8,813	12,504	12,870
Participation rate (percent)	54.3	54.0	58.0	64.8	65.7

Note: Data in this and most other tables in this chapter are from two sources; those for 1951, 1961, 1971, and 1981 are from censuses, those for 1986 from the labour force survey. Survey data are less accurate than census data.

Sources: Statistics Canada Catalogues 71-001, 92-915, and 94-702.

The Supply of Labour: Demographic Influences

Total labour supply depends not only on actual numbers of people of eligible age (taken as 15 or older in Canada) available, but also on the proportion of that population active in the labour force, either employed or actively looking for work; this proportion is the participation rate.

As population grows, so does labour supply. The Atlantic labour force has grown rapidly since 1951, but at a rate lower than the national level. The labour force in Canada went up at an annual average rate of 2.6% between 1951 and 1986 (Table 14.1). In the Atlantic region this was most closely approached by Newfoundland (2.2%) followed by New Brunswick (1.8%), Nova Scotia (1.7%), then Prince Edward Island

(1.6%). These lower rates are rather misleading; a long record of migration from Atlantic Canada has contributed to labour force growth in other parts of the country.

Most of the increase in labour force numbers has occurred since 1961, with Newfoundland's labour force doubling between 1961 and 1986, and increasing by 60%-70% in the other three provinces. Labour force size nationally over the same period went up by 130%, due mostly to a mixture of faster population growth and generally stronger economic performances in other parts of Canada.

Variations in the participation rate since 1951 have been responsible for quite profound changes in the structure of the labour force (Table 14.1). Total participation rates have increased slightly, once again especially since 1961. A complete time series over this period would reveal variations more or less in line with business cycle ups and downs. Participation rates in Atlantic Canada remain below those for Canada as a whole.

The backbone of these labour force figures is one rather complex phenomenon - the Baby Boom. The years between 1946 and 1966 saw great natural increases in the Canadian population, supplemented at various times by waves of immigration from other countries. As the children born during this period have grown and matured, they have entered the labour force to look for work. The first members of the Baby Boom reached labour force age in 1961; between 1961 and 1971, the proportion of the labour force aged between 15 and 24 went up from 24% to 28%. As all Baby Boomers grow older, they will significantly influence the course of the Canadian economy well into the next century.

Since 1971, this "youth bubble" has been entering the so-called prime age groups, those between 25 and 54 years old, and they will continue to do so for the balance of the century. Whereas the 15-to-24 age group expanded between 1961 and 1971, the 25-to-54 age group is now expanding. Workers aged 55 or over are taking up a smaller proportion of the work force. Since the recession of 1982, in particular, many older workers have chosen to take early retirement to help industries adjust to changing structures.

The Supply of Labour: Males and Females

In the total participation rate increases since 1951, the male participation rate has declined slightly while the female participation rate has increased dramatically (Figure 14.1). For example, in 1951 in Prince Edward Island, only 19% of eligible females were in the labour force; by 1986, this had increased to 50%. This means that total growth in participation

FIGURE 14.1: LABOUR FORCE PARTICIPATION RATES

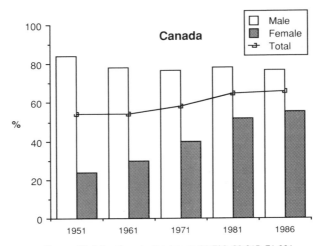

Source: Statistics Canada Catalogues 94-702, 92-915, 71-001.

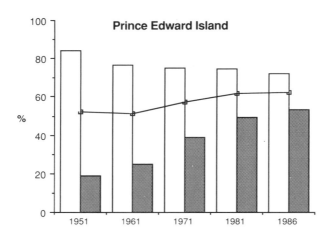

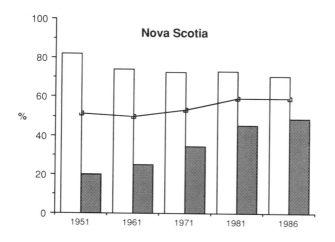

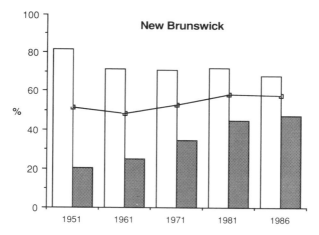

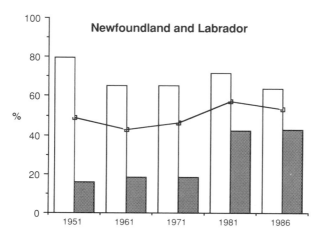

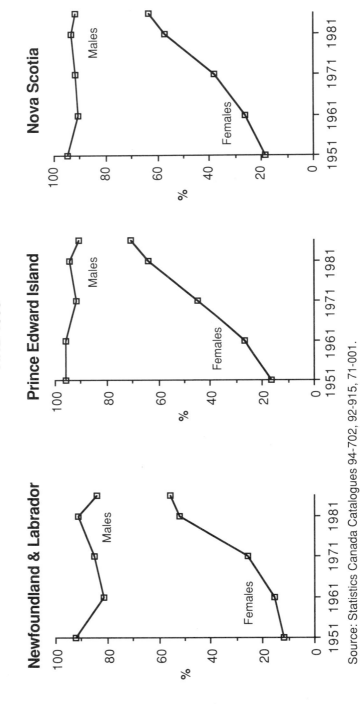

FIGURE 14.2: MALE AND FEMALE PARTICIPATION RATES 25–54 YEAR AGE GROUP, ATLANTIC PROVINCES AND CANADA, 1951, 1961, 1971, 1981, AND 1986

Source: Statistics Canada Catalogues 94-702, 92-915, 71-001.

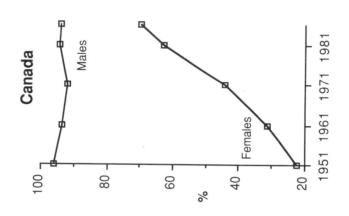

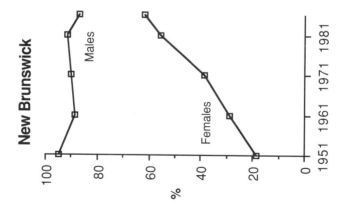

rates has been exclusively due to larger numbers of women looking for jobs.

Much of this higher participation by women has occurred in the prime age groups. In Prince Edward Island once again, only 16.4% of women aged from 25 to 54 were in the labour force in 1951. This increased to 26.6% by 1961, 45% by 1971, and 70.4% in 1986 (Figure 14.2). Indeed, this age group for both males and females records highest participation rates, with males showing slight declines since 1951, but with great increases for females.

Participation rates in different age groups demonstrate a variety of trends. Younger males (15 to 24 years old) participate less in the labour force in the 1980s than in 1951, while females in the same age group participate more. As well, the participation rate of older males (over 55 years old) has gone down steadily, whereas that of females over 55 has increased steadily. Older workers in general may have rather more choice in terms of participation. They have presumably built up a degree of security through pension funds, mortgage-free home-ownership, and so on and could effectively leave the labour force when at, or close to, official retirement age. If demand for labour picks up, however, they can also rejoin at their discretion. The same degree of flexibility is not enjoyed by prime-aged or younger workers, who face the expense of setting up homes and bringing up families. Younger single workers may exercise the option of higher education as an alternative to joining the permanent labour force, effectively delaying their entry for several years but actually entering at a higher, more assured level.

Structural shifts in composition of the labour force reflect quite radical social changes. These revolve around marital status, structure of households, access to higher education, and improved security for older people. A higher divorce rate, for example, has several ramifications. Instead of one household to support, there are now two. A single household income may, therefore, be replaced by two incomes. Even without marital breakup, there has been great growth in the number of two-income households. This has been the result of a number of factors; for example, both partners in a marriage may be highly educated, have skills and experience which are in demand, may aspire to improved material wealth or social position.

Much of the growth in female employment reflects changes in attitudes, both on the part of women themselves and on the part of society as a whole. More women have taken a conscious decision not to marry until later in life, or at least to postpone having children until they have undertaken higher education or training, or have established a career. The

TABLE 14.2: PERCENTAGE DISTRIBUTION OF POPULATION 15 YEARS AND OLDER BY HIGHEST LEVEL OF SCHOOLING, ATLANTIC PROVINCES AND CANADA 1981

	Newfoundland and Labrador	Prince Edward Island	Nova Scotia	New Brunswick	Canada
	– percent of total –				
Elementary-secondary:					
0-8 years	30.1	23.5	20.3	27.9	20.1
9-completion	28.9	31.4	33.9	28.8	27.9
Vocational training trade certificate or diploma	2.1	2.6	3.5	2.8	3.4
High school certificate	10.2	8.3	7.9	10.9	13.0
Other non-university education:					
Without trade certificate or diploma	3.0	4.5	3.7	3.5	6.0
With trade certificate or diploma	9.9	7.6	9.4	6.5	6.5
With other certificate or diploma	3.4	6.1	5.8	6.2	7.2
University:					
Without degree	7.4	9.9	8.0	7.3	7.9
With degree	4.7	6.1	7.4	6.1	8.0

Source: Statistics Canada 92-921

growth in service industries, especially, has been instrumental in the growth of female employment.

The Supply of Labour: Education and Training

Education is vital to career development, and measures in broad terms the quality of labour supply. The educational status of the Atlantic labour force falls below that of Canada (Table 14.2). The region has a higher proportion of its labour force age population with only elementary education (up to Grade 8), although the proportion completing high school is close to national averages. There are relatively fewer people with trade certificates or diplomas, and fewer university students who have actually obtained degrees.

There have been great improvements in education levels since the early 1960s in Atlantic Canada, however, and many who have received training in the region now ply their trades in other parts of Canada. In 1961, more than 40% of the labour force population had only elementary levels of education, and less than 8% had any university training. By 1981, these proportions were 30% and 11% respectively.

TABLE 14.3: EMPLOYMENT, ATLANTIC PROVINCES AND CANADA, 1951, 1961, 1971, 1981, AND 1986

	Year	Total	Male	Female
Newfoundland and Labrador:	1951	101,123	84,323	16,800
	1961	104,037	80,933	23,104
	1971	137,635	98,685	38,955
	1981	186,725	118,500	68,220
	1986	181,000	109,000	72,000
Prince Edward Island:	1951	33,695	27,795	5,900
	1961	33,436	25,496	7,940
	1971	41,090	27,515	13,565
	1981	49,595	30,000	19,595
	1986	52,000	29,000	22,000
Nova Scotia:	1951	215,084	173,042	42,042
	1961	228,551	171,582	56,969
	1971	268,325	182,710	85,620
	1981	340,760	210,215	130,540
	1986	344,000	199,000	146,000
New Brunswick:	1951	165,142	131,613	33,529
	1961	169,154	124,306	44,848
	1971	208,490	140,880	67,615
	1981	260,990	160,200	100,790
	1986	267,000	153,000	114,000
Canada:	1951	5,208,096	4,057,987	1,150,109
	1961	6,259,452	4,531,207	1,728,245
	1971	8,117,380	5,335,600	2,781,785
	1981	11,167,915	6,693,220	4,474,700
	1986	11,634,000	6,657,000	4,977,000

Sources: Statistics Canada Catalogues 71-001, 92-915, and 94-702.

The Demand for Labour

Rapid economic expansion in the post-war period has seen the number of jobs in Atlantic Canada expand remarkably, particularly since 1961. Total employment went up by an annual average rate of 2.2% in Newfoundland between 1961 and 1986, 1.8% in Prince Edward Island, 1.6% in Nova Scotia, and 1.8% in New Brunswick; the increase nationally was 2.6% (Table 14.3). Jobs held by women went up at much faster rates than those held by men. Women held only 19% of all jobs in the region in 1951, but held 42% in 1986. Even as total employment dropped during the early 1980s, female employment continued to grow; all of the decline involved male jobs. Much of the total growth in employment since 1971 has involved females taking jobs (Figure 14.3).

Aspects of demand for labour include the rising incidence of part-time

Atlantic Canada Today

FIGURE 14.3: EMPLOYMENT CHANGES, ATLANTIC CANADA 1951, 1961, 1971, 1981, AND 1975–1986

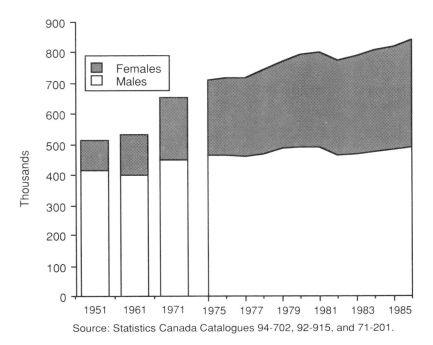

Source: Statistics Canada Catalogues 94-702, 92-915, and 71-201.

work, and increased seasonality of employment. In 1975, 67,000 people in the region worked less than 30 hours a week; by 1986, this number had increased to 124,000, or some 15% of all jobs. About 70% of all part-time jobs are held by women, accounting for about 25% of all female employment in the three Maritime provinces, and about 20% in Newfoundland. A greater degree of part-time work among women may explain why female employment has always increased in recent years although male employment may have declined.

Seasonality of employment is particularly noticeable in areas where fishing and tourism dominate, such as Newfoundland and Prince Edward Island (Table 14.4). Seasonality increases, as well, in agricultural areas where much of the harvest must be completed in a short period. There has been a tradition of rotating between occupations in many parts of Atlantic Canada, especially between forestry, farming and fishing. This link to a simpler, less commercial lifestyle than exists in the 1980s has almost disppeared. Some fishermen may still run a few head of cattle, and farmers still cut a few cords of pulpwood from woodlots in winter. Dependence on seasonal rotation has declined as income maintenance programs, such as unemployment insurance, have increased.

Labour Markets   **167**

TABLE 14.4: AVERAGE SEASONAL VARIATION[1] IN EMPLOYMENT, ATLANTIC PROVINCES AND CANADA, SELECTED YEARS 1966–1986

	1966	1975	1977	1980	1983	1986
	– percent –					
Newfoundland and Labrador	7.4	7.0	6.2	7.7	8.2	7.8
Prince Edward Island	7.4	11.0	8.5	8.1	8.2	8.7
Nova Scotia	4.6	4.5	4.0	4.0	4.5	3.4
New Brunswick	4.4	5.9	6.3	5.3	6.3	5.1
Canada	3.2	2.9	3.0	2.5	2.9	2.1

Note: 1) Measured by the monthly mean percentage deviation from the annual employment trend. The larger the value, the greater the seasonal variation.

Sources: Statistics Canada Catalogues 71-001, 71-201

TABLE 14.5: UNEMPLOYMENT RATE, ATLANTIC PROVINCES AND CANADA, 1966–1986

	Newfoundland and Labrador	Prince Edward Island	Nova Scotia	New Brunswick	Canada
	– percent of labour force –				
1966	5.8	—	4.7	5.3	3.4
1967	5.9	—	4.9	5.2	3.8
1968	7.1	—	5.1	5.7	4.5
1969	7.4	—	4.9	6.7	4.4
1970	7.3	—	5.3	6.3	5.7
1971	8.4	—	7.0	6.1	6.2
1972	9.2	10.8	7.0	7.0	6.2
1973	10.0	—	6.6	7.7	5.5
1974	13.0	—	6.8	7.5	5.3
1975	14.0	8.0	7.7	9.8	6.9
1976	13.3	9.6	9.5	11.0	7.1
1977	15.5	9.8	10.6	13.2	8.1
1978	16.2	9.8	10.5	12.5	8.3
1979	15.1	11.2	10.1	11.1	7.4
1980	13.3	10.6	9.7	11.0	7.5
1981	13.9	11.2	10.2	11.5	7.5
1982	16.8	12.9	13.2	14.0	11.0
1983	18.8	12.2	13.2	14.8	11.9
1984	20.5	12.8	13.1	14.9	11.3
1985	21.3	13.2	13.8	15.2	10.5
1986	20.0	13.4	13.4	14.4	9.6

Note: Not available for Prince Edward Island in most years before 1975.

Source: Statistics Canada Catalogue 71-201

TABLE 14.6: AVERAGE ANNUAL YOUTH UNEMPLOYMENT RATE, ATLANTIC PROVINCES AND CANADA, SELECTED YEARS 1975–1986

	1975	1979	1981	1984	1986
	– percent of labour force aged 15–24 –				
Newfoundland and Labrador	22.7	25.3	24.5	34.1	31.1
Nova Scotia	14.1	18.6	17.3	21.7	21.4
New Brunswick	15.0	18.5	19.4	23.9	22.9
Canada	12.0	12.9	13.2	17.9	15.2

Note: Data are not available for Prince Edward Island.

Source: Statistics Canada Catalogue 71-201

Seasonal employment opportunities are important to younger people, such as students in summer, and appear to be more typical of male employment than female. This is probably because many seasonal resource industries are dominated by male employment, whereas year-round work (such as that in offices and stores) is more typical of female employment.

Self-employment has been a rising component of total employment in Atlantic Canada over the years. It accounts for as many as one in five of all jobs in Prince Edward Island, where there are relatively high numbers of primary producers such as farmers and fishermen. However, more high-income professionals in the region, including solidly increasing numbers of women, have set up their own businesses. Self-employment may be motivated by the desire to be one's own boss, or lack of opportunities to rise in paid employment within a company; or it may be a response to losing paid employment and being thrown on one's own resources by necessity.

Unemployment: An Imbalance Between Demand and Supply

The single theme which most frequently arises in discussions of the Atlantic economy and its labour markets is the persistence of high unemployment. Each of the four provinces has traditionally had higher unemployment rates than Canada as a whole, and the gap has tended to increase over the years (Table 14.5). As mentioned in Chapter 10, unemployment itself has become a measure of regional disparity. There are numerous aspects to this enormous problem.

Youth Unemployment. Although youth unemployment is a pressing social concern across Canada, the situation in Atlantic Canada is particularly urgent (Table 14.6). More than one in five young poeople were officially unemployed in Atlantic Canada in 1986, a proportion that rises close to one in three in Newfoundland. These official statistics probably understate the true extent of the problem, as many people have despaired of ever finding work, have effectively left the labour force, and therefore escape official enumeration.

The problem of youth unemployment has been aggravated by the loss of such traditional outlets as job opportunities in other parts of the country, particularly for unskilled workers. It has become particularly difficult for young people to find that first important job, where they can start accumulating skills and experience.

Geographical Distribution of Unemployment. Within Atlantic Canada there are areas and localities with even higher unemployment rates than provincial averages indicate. While places like Halifax have jobless rates around national averages, other local economies are much worse off. The west coast of Newfoundland and Labrador, for example, saw about 23% of its workforce unemployed in 1986 compared with a provincial average of 20%, and 17.6% in St John's. Lower participation rates probably mask worse problems. Northeastern Nova Scotia (including Cape Breton Island) saw 23% of its labour force unemployed in 1986 compared with 9.9% in Halifax County. Northeastern New Brunswick had 19% of its labour force unemployed compared with 11% in the area that includes Fredericton.

Unemployment and Education. There is strong evidence that unemployment declines as levels of education increase. In Nova Scotia in 1986, for example, some 20% of those whose education stopped at Grade 8 were unemployed compared with 10% of those with some kind of post-secondary qualification (Table 14.7). At the national level, unemployment is lowest among university graduates. The better educated a person is, the easier it is to find work.

The issue is not simple, however, and discussion centres on whether the educational system is equipping people with the right skills to find work, particularly during a period of rapid technological change. New technologies require training in non-traditional occupations, and also require adaptation to traditional sectors. In circumstances such as these, is it better to provide highly specific educational training with the risk that demand for certain skills may evaporate, or to provide a good, broadly based education that allows people to be flexible, and quick to learn new skills?

Income Support Programs. Canadian society is in the privileged situation of being wealthy and organised enough to afford a wide range of

TABLE 14.7: UNEMPLOYMENT RATE BY EDUCATIONAL ATTAINMENT, ATLANTIC PROVINCES AND CANADA, 1986

	Newfoundland and Labrador	Prince Edward Island	Nova Scotia	New Brunswick	Canada
	— percent of labour force —				
Up to 8 years of high school	28.0	—	20.0	21.6	12.2
Some or all secondary, but no post-secondary	23.0	14.0	15.0	16.7	11.4
Some post secondary	—	—	12.6	—	8.9
Post-secondary certificate or diploma	14.5	—	10.1	—	6.6
University degree	—	—	—	—	4.6
Average	20.0	13.4	13.4	14.4	9.6

Note: Some data are not available because the small sample size makes them too unreliable.

Source: Statistics Canada 71-001

income support to individuals. These include unemployment insurance. It can be argued that the effects of such a program are to keep people tied to low-income, low-productivity jobs rather than encouraging them to change to other occupations or to move to parts of the country where jobs are available. Excess labour is thereby retained in activities that may be fundamentally uneconomic.

Unemployment insurance beneficiaries are more common in Atlantic Canada that elsewhere in the country (Table 14.8). Even when economic conditions have been generally healthy, the four provinces have had a greater percentage of their labour force receiving unemployment benefits, particularly in those parts where seasonality of employment is higher.

A Note on Organised Labour.

Atlantic Canada has a tradition of connections to organised labour, and membership in unions continues to grow. Total membership in the region went up from 103,734 in 1962 to 272,385 in 1984, or by an annual average rate of 4.5%. Types of union membership have changed over the years, with the influence of international unions (based in the United States) tending to go down, and membership in public sector unions increasing. International unions still remain important in Newfoundland and Nova Scotia, and public-sector unions most important in Prince Edward Island.

TABLE 14.8: BENEFICIARIES OF REGULAR UNEMPLOYMENT INSURANCE, ATLANTIC PROVINCES AND CANADA 1976–1986

	Newfoundland and Labrador	Prince Edward Island	Nova Scotia	New Brunswick	Canada
	— percent of labour force —				
1976	20.3	14.2	9.4	14.7	6.1
1977	20.4	14.6	10.7	15.8	6.4
1978	21.4	14.8	10.8	15.7	6.5
1979	19.1	13.0	9.4	14.0	5.5
1980	18.0	11.9	8.7	13.3	5.2
1981	18.4	13.3	9.1	14.0	5.2
1982	22.3	16.1	12.5	17.5	8.6
1983	23.8	16.5	12.6	18.0	9.2
1984	30.1	22.2	12.7	21.5	8.3
1985	28.6	22.2	12.1	19.8	8.1
1986	29.5	21.1	12.0	18.5	7.7

Source: Statistics Canada Catalogue 71-201 and 73-001

TABLE 14.9: AVERAGE WEEKLY EARNINGS, ATLANTIC PROVINCES (INDUSTRIAL AGGREGATES) AND CANADA (BY SECTOR) 1986

	— dollars —
Industrial aggregate	430.88
Newfoundland and Labrador	408.44
Prince Edward Island	348.10
Nova Scotia	390.33
New Brunswick	399.94
Forestry	567.38
Mines, quarries and oil wells	710.94
Manufacturing	504.48
Construction	509.73
Transportation, communications and utilities	559.02
Trade	317.30
Finance, insurance and real estate	452.35
Community, business and personal services	364.34
Public administration	545.36

Source: Statistics Canada Catalogue 72-002

Newfoundland has the highest proportion of its labour force unionised, amounting to about 37% in 1984. Membership in the other provinces has also been increasing as a proportion of the labour force. Prince Edward Island saw increases in the 1970s, mostly as the Comprehensive Development Plan brought greater numbers of government-related jobs.

Wage levels in Atlantic Canada tend to fall short of national averages (Table 14.9). A higher-than-average incidence of high-wage industries (such as mining) pulls the averages of Newfoundland and New Brunswick upwards, and the greater incidence of service industries in the other two provinces probably depresses their industrial aggregate wage.

Policies to Address Unemployment

The mix of problems that produces stubbornly high unemployment rates in Atlantic Canada is probably the most serious facing the region in the late twentieth century. Unemployment has remained high (and participation rates low) in spite of a series of policy measures over the years. As long as there is a pool of unused labour in the region, incomes will remain low, there will be little incentive to undertake job enhancement training, the region will be typified by low productivity, and a "dependence mentality" will be fostered.

Since high levels of unemployment are related to most other facets of economic endeavour, measures to address unemployment must cross a broad spectrum of policies. Regional development policies, designed to increase and diversify the region's economic base and thereby create stable jobs, enter the equation. Fiscal policies also play a part, as they contain the incentives whereby governments attract industries and ensure them an equable atmosphere for investment.

Manpower policies are vital. They embrace job training, which should extend as far as management training to provide a supply of administrative and entrepreneurial skills. Policies to improve job skills are particularly important in the late 1980s, a time of rapid technological change and unacceptably high unemployment amongst young people. The ability to identify the timing of change will, in large part, dictate any productivity improvements in the region in both traditional and new industries.

Further Reading

Betcherman, G., *Meeting Skill Requirements: Report of the Human Resources Survey.* Prepared for the Economic Council of Canada. Ottawa, 1982.

Boulet, J-A and L. Lavallee, *The Changing Economic Status of Women*. Prepared for the Economic Council of Canada. Ottawa, 1984.

Commission of Inquiry on Unemployment Insurance, *Report*. C.E. Forget, Chairman. Ottawa, 1986.

Economic Council of Canada, *In Short Supply: Jobs and Skills in the 1980s*. Ottawa,1982.

Employment and Immigration Canada, *Learning a Living in Canada*. Report to the Minister of Employment and Immigration by the Skill Development Leave Task Force. Ottawa, 1983. Two Volumes.

Royal Commission on Employment and Unemployment, *Building on our Strengths: Final Report*. J.D. House, Chairman, St John's 1986.

CHAPTER 15

Export Trade:
The Global Marketplace

Canada is a trading nation whose relative degree of prosperity has always depended on selling in markets much larger than those offered by the country's own population. This applies especially to Atlantic Canada, where regional markets alone would be insufficient to support growth. In the late twentieth century, these truths apply even more than in the past.

Atlantic exports in 1986 were worth $6.3 billion, marking an annual average increase of 12.2% since 1965 in nominal terms (Table 15.1). Even in real terms, the value of exports in 1986 was almost 3.5 times greater than in 1965. Value of exports dropped sharply in the early 1980s as recession took hold. Many of Atlantic Canada's exports are resource-based, making them particularly vulnerable to ups and downs in the business cycle; there has been a slower recovery from recession in the mid-1980s in the region than for Canada as a whole.

What Determines that Trade Occurs?

Trade analysis has become a specialised branch of economics. Determination of trading patterns involves many considerations: relative costs of production in different countries; resource and manufacturing structures; location; changes in relative exchange rates; barriers to trade; changes in aggregate demand, and many other factors.

TABLE 15.1: VALUE OF ATLANTIC EXPORTS, 1965 TO 1986

	Thousands of Current Dollars	Thousands of Constant (1971) Dollars	As a Proportion of Canadian Total %
1965	561,903	610,101	6.6
1966	737,384	781,955	7.3
1967	708,029	744,510	6.4
1968	811,565	843,623	6.1
1969	800,353	819,194	5.6
1970	989,243	983,343	6.0
1971	1,017,397	1,017,397	5.9
1972	1,091,701	1,056,826	5.6
1973	1,490,799	1,261,251	6.0
1974	2,042,372	1,299,219	6.5
1975	2,110,317	1,218,428	6.5
1976	2,332,826	1,322,464	6.2
1977	2,746,670	1,455,575	6.3
1978	3,220,699	1,568,777	6.2
1979	4,543,225	1,827,524	7.1
1980	4,934,781	1,706,356	6.6
1981	5,321,654	1,730,619	6.6
1982	4,103,175	1,323,178	5.0
1983	4,197,422	1,371,258	4.8
1984	5,045,422	1,625,982	4.6
1985	5,245,478	1,650,559	4.5
1986	6,288,878	2,046,495	5.4

Note: Totals in this table have been adjusted to reflect trans-shipment of those products which originate in other parts of Canada through Atlantic ports, such as Prairie grains at Halifax and Saint John. The figures also incorporate estimates of exports of Labrador iron ore, which in official statistics appear as exports from Quebec because of trans-shipment at Sept-Iles.

Sources: Statistics Canada Catalogue 65-001 and special tabulations, adjusted by the Atlantic Provinces Economic Council.

The earliest concept of trade identified a society's wealth with the acquisition of, and control over, a limited global supply of precious resources. This was called mercantilism. The import of goods was regarded as a wealth-draining process, and mercantilists encouraged protection of domestic industry to avoid this.

A different image of trade appeared from the writings of Adam Smith, who measured wealth in terms of all goods rather than just commodities such as gold. Smith rejected protectionism, considering it an impediment to the natural and most efficient allocation of resources through the process of trade. His analysis of trade in this way is closely in line with his theories of the efficiencies of the division of labour. His ideas were taken further by another classical economist, David Ricardo, who formulated the theory of comparative advantage. This is the cornerstone of trade theory.

Comparative advantage basically states that a country concentrates on producing those things it does best, and engages in trade to obtain other things it wants or needs. If Canada, for example, were three times more efficient in producing fish than Britain, but only two times more efficient in producing steel, it would have a comparative advantage in producing fish. It would make sense, therefore, for Canada to concentrate its efforts in fish production and to obtain its supplies of steel from Britain. Both economies would benefit from this trade, although both would still retain the ability to produce that item (fish or steel) it obtains more cheaply from the other.

Trends in Atlantic Exports

Resource-based production accounts for about 90% of exports originating in Atlantic Canada. In some cases, this involves export of resources more or less as raw materials, with little or no processing within the region. In many more cases, a degree of processing takes place within the region, but the exports themselves undergo further processing, usually into consumer-ready end products, at destination. This means that varying degrees of value-added attached to the region's resources do not stay in the region.

There has been quite impressive growth in the value of Atlantic exports since 1965 in both nominal and real terms. The largest share has been claimed by the commodity group inedible fabricated materials, with exports of such items as forest products, electricity, and refined petroleum products (Figure 15.1). There have also been good increases in the value of other important groups of commodities, especially food products and inedible end products. Each major group deserves brief mention.

Food, feed, beverages and tobacco exports were valued at $1.8 billion in 1986, a very strong increase since the 1970s (Figure 15.2). The group includes such familiar Atlantic Canadian products as fish (some 80%-90% of the group total each year since 1977), and agricultural products (both fresh and processed). There is also export of beer to American markets, a development of the 1980s. Most food-related exports go to American markets, while some higher-value fish products (such as live lobster or other fresh fish) are sent all over the world.

Inedible crude materials are mostly minerals and items such as logs. They have occupied a generally declining proportion of total exports

FIGURE 15.1: VALUE OF EXPORTS BY MAJOR COMMODITY GROUP, ATLANTIC CANADA, AND VALUE OF THE CANADIAN DOLLAR IN U.S. FUNDS, 1965–1985

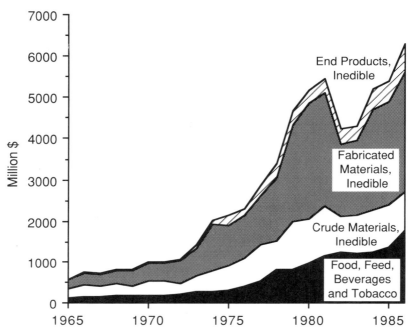

Value of the Canadian Dollar 1965-1985

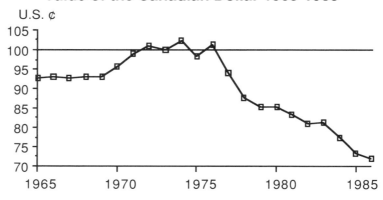

Source: Statistics Canada, Special Tabulations; Bank of Canada.

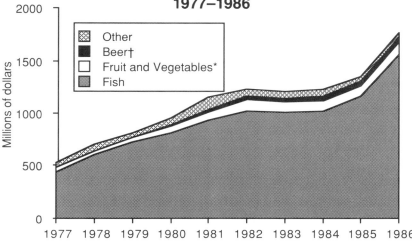

FIGURE 15.2: SOME DETAILS OF ATLANTIC FOOD, FEED, BEVERAGES AND TOBACCO EXPORTS 1977–1986

Notes: † Classified as "fermented alcoholic beverages" in the statistics.
* Mainly potatoes (both seed and table stock); apples; blueberries; and frozen end products.

Source: Statistics Canada, special tabulation.

FIGURE 15.3: SOME DETAILS OF ATLANTIC EXPORTS OF INEDIBLE CRUDE MATERIALS, 1977–1986

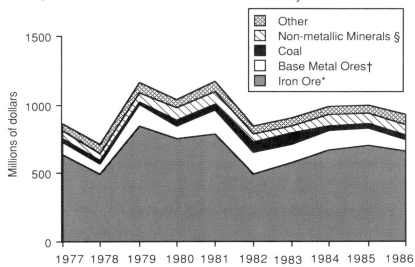

Notes: § Mainly unmanufactured asbestos and gypsum.
† Lead, zinc and copper.   * Ores, concentrates and scrap.

Source: Statistics Canada, special tabulations.

over the years, but were still worth almost $1 billion to the Atlantic economy in 1986 (Figure 15.3). The group had a peak between 1979 and 1981, record years for iron ore shipments. Recession in the early 1980s severely affected iron ore markets, which rely heavily on sales to North American steel mills. Other important products are base metal ores (zinc, copper and lead); non-metallic minerals such as gypsum and asbestos; coal, and logs.

Inedible fabricated materials exports include some of the region's most important products: pulp and paper, lumber, petroleum products, and electricity. There are links, as well, to mining, reflected in the exports of chemical elements (phosphorus from Newfoundland); fertilisers (potash and diammonium phosphate from New Brunswick); and lead metal. Total value of these products in 1986 approached $3 billion (Figure 15.4). Some 60% of this total were pulp and paper products, with a further substantial, but rather variable, proportion of refined petroleum products (mostly gasoline and heating oil) .[1] Electricity exports developed in the early 1970s when generating capacity in New Brunswick expanded.

Inedible end products are the exports with the greatest amount of value-added. Even though in 1986 they account for only about 11% of total exports in the region, this is a substantial improvement since 1970, for example, when they accounted for less than 3%. Much of the growth in the group has come from tire production in Nova Scotia, but the array of products represented is wide, ranging from navigational equipment to motor vehicles, eyeglass frames, pharmaceutical and medical products, and electronic products. Since these products are higher in value and generally lower in bulk than resource-based goods, they cost relatively less to ship.

About 65% of Atlantic exports went to American markets in 1986. This is a smaller proportion than Canada's 80% or so, an amount heavily weighted by export of cars and trucks from southern Ontario to the United States (a trade governed by the terms of the Auto Pact), and substantial exports of resource-based products (including oil and gas) from the western provinces. Atlantic Canada's proximity to Europe has historically seen a proportionally greater amount of shipments to trans-Atlantic markets. This share has declined slightly over the years of consolidation and enlargement of the European Economic Community (EEC), a group of countries with the aim of promoting trade between themselves to the exclusion of non-Community trade.

Types of exports vary between provinces (Table 15.2). Newfoundland's exports are heavily dominated by minerals (mostly iron ore), fish prod-

TABLE 15.4: SOME DETAILS OF ATLANTIC EXPORTS OF INEDIBLE FABRICATED MATERIALS, 1977–1986

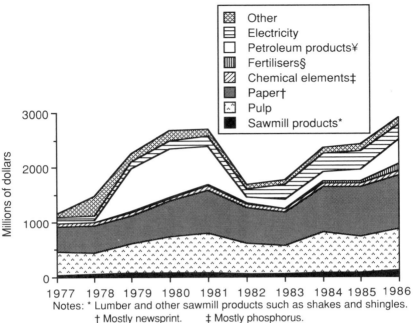

Notes: * Lumber and other sawmill products such as shakes and shingles.
      † Mostly newsprint.   ‡ Mostly phosphorus.
      § Diammonium phosphate to 1983, combined with potash since then.
      ¥ Gasoline and fuel oil.
Source: Statistics Canada, special tabulations.

TABLE 15.2: EXPORTS BY PRINCIPAL COMMODITY GROUP, ATLANTIC PROVINCES AND CANADA, 1986

	Food, Feed Beverages and Tobacco	Inedible Crude Materials	Inedible Fabricated Materials	Inedible End Products	Total
	– $'000 –				
	– (percent of total) –				
Newfoundland and Labrador	557,539	691,154	384,800	7,644	1,641,137
	(34.0)	(42.1)	(23.4)	(0.5)	(100.0)
Prince Edward Island	124,804	4,217	1,422	15,713	146,156
	(85.4)	(2.9)	(1.0)	(10.7)	(100.0)
Nova Scotia	679,064	99,647	529,268	607,985	1,915,964
	(35.4)	(5.2)	(27.6)	(31.7)	(100.0)
New Brunswick	405,278	135,389	1,991,783	53,171	2,585,621
	(15.7)	(5.2)	(77.0)	(2.1)	(100.0)
Atlantic Canada	1,766,685	930,407	2,907,273	684,513	6,288,878
	(28.1)	(14.8)	(46.2)	(10.9)	(100.0)
Canada	9,582,842	15,314,039	38,343,208	52,649,827	116,159,916
	(8.2)	(13.2)	(33.0)	(45.3)	(100.0)

Source: Statistics Canada, special tabulations.

ucts, and newsprint. Exports of inedible end products accounted for less than 0.5% in 1986. Prince Edward Island's exports are predominantly agricultural in nature (mostly potatoes) with fish also being important. The Island has a healthy 11% or so of its exports in the inedible end products category, including ophthalmic goods and medical products.

The greatest diversity of exports is found in Nova Scotia, where some 32% of the value in 1986 was in inedible end products, a figure heavily influenced by tire production. New Brunswick's exports, the most important of which are forest products, food products, minerals, and electricity, lead the region in terms of value.

There are many institutional factors that influence the flows of trade. Large parts of Atlantic Canada's pulp and paper making capacity, for example, are integrated with other mills, under the same ownership but sometimes located in other countries. Pulp manufactured at an Atlantic mill is frequently shipped thousands of miles away for further manufacture into paper. While most of the region's fish exported to the United States goes to Boston, this is not because New England is its final destination, but because the Boston fish market is a continental clearing house for fish products.

Exchange Rates: A Note

Variation in exchange rates is an important determinant of export success, especially if the exports themselves tend to be lower-value products. A movement of a cent or two in the relative values of the Canadian and American dollars has important effects. If the Canadian dollar loses some ground, American buyers pay less for Canadian imports, and vice versa. Much of the impressive increases in Canadian exports to American markets since the early 1970s can be attributed to a succession of declines in the value of the Canadian dollar against its American counterpart (see lower part of Figure 15.1).

Fluctuation of other exchange rates influences export sales, particularly in highly competitive markets. Scandinavian producers of fish and forest products, for example, have periodically "invaded" Canadian export markets both in Europe and the United States, aided by substantial devaluations of their currencies. Occasionally, such devaluations have been a conscious policy on the part of exporting countries in efforts to increase foreign sales.

Movements between the North American currencies often see one losing ground against the other, itself an important influence on bilateral trade. Sometimes they move more or less in concert relative to other major currencies. When the Canadian dollar lost 5.5% of its value against the American dollar in 1984, for example, other major currencies lost more (the Swiss franc 10%, the German mark 16.4%, the Japanese yen 18%, the British pound 20.5%, and the French franc 33.1%). In European terms, therefore, the Canadian dollar remained relatively strong because of its close linkage to the American dollar. This meant that Canadian exporters found it more difficult to compete in European markets and that Canada's most important export market (the United States) could be served more easily by European producers.

Barriers to Trade

Trade rarely moves completely freely from country to country.[2] Barriers to trade are devices that have been invoked for one or more reasons: to protect domestic industries from import competition in a situation of aggregate oversupply; to foster new industries towards a state of competitiveness; to assure an adequate domestic supply of products deemed important to national wellbeing or security; or to retaliate against the protectionist moves of other countries.

The commonest barriers to trade have been tariffs, a tax on traded goods (usually imports), and quotas, quantitative restrictions on traded goods (once again, usually imports). Both raise the price of the product for the consumer. If barriers to trade become structural features of an economy, they can severely impair the abilities of industries to increase productivity, since they restrict competition, and inhibit reallocation of resources from dying industries to emerging ones.

The General Agreement on Tariffs and Trade (GATT) was established in the late 1940s, mainly to reduce levels of tariffs affecting world trade. A succession of "rounds" in the time since then has seen many tariffs reduced; the Canadian general tariff has come down from an average of between 25% and 40% in the late 1940s to about 5% or 6% in the late 1980s, though this average masks wide variations from product to product. Some labour-intensive industries in Canada are still highly protected behind tariff walls, including many textile and clothing products. Other principal trading nations which are members of GATT have also experienced reductions in levels of tariffs.

As tariffs have come down, a complex range of so-called non-tariff barriers (NTBs) has arisen. In part, these have been designed to replace tariffs, especially where removal or reduction of a tariff has had a greater-than-anticipated negative effect on domestic industry. In part, they have arisen from the increased involvement of government in many fields of economic activity. This has resulted in a plethora of policies, some of which affect traded commodities implicitly and explicitly. Examples include regional development policies, transportation subsidies, government procurement regulations, border inspection procedures, and the awarding of defence contracts.

The rise of NTBs has coincided with other developments that affect global trade in the 1980s. Trading blocs such as the EEC exist solely to promote intra-Community trade to the exclusion, if necessary, of trade with non-Community countries. The so-called newly industrialising countries have greatly increased their manufacture of a wide range of mass-produced items for markets in the industrialised world. This has been made possible, in part, by lower wages in these countries. Japan's innovation in production-line techniques has allowed more efficient production of many items, once again aimed at markets in North America and Europe. Less-developed countries have become major sources of basic resources.

These changes in trading patterns have affected manufacturing capacity in the United States, where many old-established industries with their thousands of jobs find themselves threatened by new, low-cost competition from overseas. In these circumstances, there have been many calls for some protection from imports, and trade-remedy legislation has increasingly characterised American commerce. Atlantic products affected include groundfish, lumber, hogs and pork, potatoes, tires, and potash. There are constant rumblings about extending the list to include other products such as newsprint, where a case would be made that federal-provincial incentives to assist mill modernisation in the 1970s and 1980s effectively amounts to a subsidy on exports of pulp and paper, and therefore constitutes an NTB.

Free Trade with the United States

Few topics receive more emotional debate in Canada than the negotiation of a free trade agreement with the United States. Free trade with the United States is older than Confederation itself, as the British North American colonies had reciprocity up to 1866. Confederation, indeed, was a response to losing access to American markets, and loss of British imperial preference in trade. Sir Wilfrid Laurier lost the 1911 election mainly because of strong nationalist sentiment against his free trade initiative. There has always been a fear in Canada of economic and cultural domination by the United States; people fear it would lead to political absorption.

The rise of protectionist sentiment in the 1980s, however, has brought back the issue of free trade, and negotiations to reach an agreement

184

began in late 1985. In fact, most Canadian exports to the United States already enter mostly free of barriers, although contingency actions in the 1980s have seen this overall pattern subject to more restrictions. Resource-based exports especially have almost unencumbered access to American markets. In general, the less processing a resource receives in Canada, the lower the barriers to its entering American markets. Atlantic frozen fish blocks, for example, face few American barriers and receive further processing at American plants. Fish sticks, however, face a duty of 10%, a significant margin for a relatively low-value product.

Most theoretical work on the economic impact of free trade reveals that Canadian industry would benefit in aggregate. Much Canadian industry has developed behind protective barriers; these have fostered relatively small, high cost, inefficient plants with limited production runs geared to supplying domestic markets. Removal of these barriers to trade with the United States would allow Canadian industries to invest in more efficient plants to compete with lower-cost imports and to take advantage of assured access to a much bigger market. Establishment of a bilateral dispute-settlement body would allow Canada direct access to mediation and solution of trade conflicts with the Americans, rather than being on the outside or the fringes of American domestic trade remedy procedures, as is now the case.

Free trade would also allow some further local resource-based production. In Atlantic Canada, this would especially affect fish-processing, meaning extra value-added and jobs. Other, non-resource-based industries would benefit from specialised production, aimed at fairly small but stable and high value market niches. Consumers in general would benefit from lower prices and higher real incomes as more efficient plants improved productivity.

However, there is no doubt the industrial adjustment required to achieve these benefits would be substantial, and more painful for some industries than others. A comprehensive set of adjustment and transitional policies and programs to assist individuals, industries, and regions to cope with the change would have to be developed. Certain sectors, especially agriculture, would be particularly vulnerable if free trade involved dismantling of supply management systems, regarded as NTBs. Important parts of Atlantic manufacturing (brewing, production of confectionery and knitwear, some fruit and vegetable processing, some furniture making, printing and publishing, boat-building) have developed behind a variety of trade barriers, which have fostered relatively small-scale plants. Exposure to low-cost American imports would entail substantial rationalisation in parts or all of these industries.

There are further problems surrounding regional development programs, originally designed to assist the less fortunate parts of Canada. Such policies have been particular targets of American trade remedy actions on the grounds they confer subsidies on exported products, and therefore give Canadian exporters an unfair competitive advantage. Removal of these incentives under free trade (on the grounds they are NTBs) would also remove a cherished source of investment and assistance in Atlantic Canada.

Trade in services has also become an issue. Canadian cultural industries, and by extension the national identity, have long been hard-pressed to survive in the face of pervasive American influences via such media as magazines and television. Regulations have been devised to extend a measure of protection to some of these industries, and removal of this protection is regarded as a very serious threat to sovereignty.

It is impossible to simplify free trade. It remains a fact, however, that Canada is the only major industrialised economy in the late 1980s without either a big domestic market and/or assured access to a big foreign market. In economic terms, there is little doubt that there will be eventual benefits from free trade; great dissension emerges over the path the national economy must tread to realise these gains.

Export Trade: An Assessment

Much of Canada's prosperity today is based firmly on ability and success in selling in international markets. This has been assisted by a generous and diverse resource endowment, aggressive selling, and proximity to the world's most affluent market. Canada and the United States account for the single biggest bilateral trade flow in the world. Atlantic industries have benefited from American demand for their products.

At the same time, global trading patterns are changing rapidly, with the emergence of trade in manufactured products from newly industrialising countries, the consolidation of the economic power of trading blocs, and the increased share of commodity trade originating in less developed countries. A response to these changes has seen Canada once again pursue the alternative of free trade with the United States. As in the past, this stirs intense national debate at many levels, not all of it economic in nature. However, it is difficult to ignore our dependence on American markets to sell many products, and the protectionist sentiment that threatens this trade in the late 1980s.

Global trade is more important and more competitive than ever before. New means of transportation and improved communication technology put world markets at the finger-tips of even the smallest company. Aided by easy access to world markets by either air or sea, Atlantic Canadians have a better chance than ever before to diversify their export base.

Footnotes

1. Variations in the export of refined petroleum products have largely coincided with turbulence on world oil markets, either seeing great increases or decreases in the price of oil. Although there have been solid exports at least since the early 1970s, there were big surges in exports in 1974 and 1975 at the time of the European oil embargo; in 1979, 1980, and 1981 during the Iranian crisis; and in 1985 and 1986 when the price of oil dropped sharply. Exclusion of petroleum products from the figures does not alter the overall trend of solid increases in the region's total exports, but it does mean that year-to-year fluctuations are narrower.

2. Barriers to trade are also common between the different parts of single countries, especially those with a federal system of government. Inter-provincial trade in Canada is hampered by federal and provincial regulations governing such things as fluid milk production and sales; liquor purchasing regulations which give preferred prices in stores to beer manufactured within the province of sale; government procurement practices; different provincial trucking regulations; and different provincial standards for registration of professional occupations. There is a good summary in Canada West Foundation, *The Canadian Common Market: Interprovincial Trade and International Competitiveness*. Calgary, 1985.

Further Reading

Canada West Foundation, *The Canadian Common Market: Interprovincial Trade and International Competitiveness*. Calgary, 1985.

Canada West Foundation, *Putting the Cards on the Table: Free Trade and Western Canadian Industries*. Calgary, 1986.

Economic Council of Canada, *The Bottom Line: Technology, Trade and Income Growth*. Ottawa, 1983.

External Affairs Department, *A Review of Canadian Trade Policy: A Background Document to Canadian Trade Policy for the 1980s*. Ottawa, 1983.

Moroz, A.R. and G.J. Meredith, *Economic Effects of Trade Liberalization with the USA: Evidence and Questions*. The Institute for Research on Public Policy, Discussion Paper in International Economics No 8510. Ottawa, 1985.

Lipsey, R.G. and M.G. Smith, *Taking the Initiative: Canada's Trade Options in a Turbulent World*. The C.D. Howe Institute, Observation No. 27. Montreal, Calgary, and Toronto, 1985.

Lipsey, R.G, and W. Dobson (eds.), *Shaping Comparative Advantage*. C.D. Howe Institute Policy Study No. 2. Montreal, Calgary, and Toronto, 1987.

Wonnacott, P., *The United States and Canada: The Quest for Free Trade*. Insitute for International Economics, Policy Analyses in International Economics No. 16. Washington, D.C., 1987.

CHAPTER 16

Atlantic Futures

Businesses and public agencies frequently employ specialised professionals as corporate planners. Their main task is to identify those current and forseeable trends that will have the most impact on the medium- and long-term future of their particular concern. How will low-cost manufactured imports affect their competitive position? How will Third World debt affect interest rates? How will energy prices move?

These forecasts are necessary for making long-range plans to expand, invest, borrow, or diversify. Some forecasts are easier to make than others; we know, for example, with a fair degree of accuracy what the Canadian population will be in 1995 or 2000, but we are less able to foresee what proportion will be living in Atlantic Canada. We know, also, that resource-based production will remain an important part of the regional economy, but we are less certain about the precise size of this part, or the mix between agriculture, fishing, forestry, mining, and energy.

There are several broad areas in the late 1980s that will continue to exert significant influences, direct and indirect, on the Atlantic economy in the forseeable future. At least five of these can be identified:

- Demographic developments
- Technological change
- Global market developments
- Public debt issues
- Environmental concerns

Demographic Developments

The size, composition, and income of a population affect markets, and a wide range of government-related services, plans, and projected revenues. The biggest single influence in this respect over the next few decades is a population whose median age is increasing—50% of the Canadian population in 1981 were less than 29.6 years old, 50% were more than 29.6 years old. The median age in both 1961 and 1971 was a little over 26. Older people, therefore, are forming a larger share of Canada's population. People 65 years old or more formed less than 8% of Atlantic Canada's population before the mid-1960s, but more than 10% in 1981. There is, moreover, a large number of people now 20 to 40 years old who are poised to begin retirement within the next few decades.

The effects of this aging will be enormous in terms of such things as provision of medical and other social services, and in administration of the Canada Pension Plan. Already in the late 1980s, health and social services take up very large shares of federal and provincial budgets, and treasuries are severely strained even with current populations of older people.

Demand for special gerontological services will increase, as one part of a new category of professional health-care skills. As older people eat less, demand for food may come down. With fewer young people around, school and university enrolment will come down, a phenomenon already observed in the 1980s. Fewer teachers will be required. Sources of investment will decline as old people draw on savings, pensions, or retirement funds to finance their declining years.

In many cases, older people are more likely to have paid off mortgages and have access to higher life savings. Relatively affluent seniors will seek a wider range of leisure activities. They will spend more time and money on tourism, and their preferences will be for group travel such as bus tours or cruises. Patterns of consumer demand may change, since seniors are more likely to have accumulated their store of worldly goods, and will be looking for new types of products to buy.

Regional distribution of population may also be influenced by an older age structure. People who left Atlantic Canada in earlier years to find work may decide to move back. They may see Atlantic Canada as an area with less pollution and a generally slower, more leisurely pace of life. The economic and political power of older people will increase both in Atlantic Canada and the nation as a whole.

Technological Change

The high technology revolution of the late twentieth century is a development every bit as momentous as the agricultural and industrial revolutions of previous centuries. Specific components of the new revolution include computers, information dissemination, telecommunications, and biotechnology.

Already they have had quite profound effects on modern industrial societies, and all can enhance a mature economy's ability to compete and diversify. The effect of this on Atlantic industry varies from sector to sector. Biotechnology, for example, is particularly important in renewable resource industries.

Computers, particularly micro-computers, are now regarded as indispensable parts of business life, and will achieve wider distribution as their versatility and speed of operation increase, and their prices decrease. When linked to new developments in telecommunications, these computers create a new industry of specialised information assembly, manipulation, and dissemination. This new industry is unique in that it can be located almost anywhere, as long as there is access to a modern telephone system. It could easily become a new cottage industry.

Global Market Developments

International trade is already a topic of immense importance in the late twentieth century, especially to a country like Canada, which depends on exporting for much of its progress, and on importing for many consumer and capital goods. The means of conducting this trade have improved, and forums have developed to discuss barriers to trade. Less developed countries have taken advantage of their large supplies of labour, and often ample resource endowments, to begin building industry to supply market demand in advanced countries. This will displace some domestic production, which will be unable to meet low-cost import competition effectively.

The 1980s have seen a wholesale retreat from liberalised world trade. Exports from less developed countries have increased, in part to finance interest payments on huge accumulated debt. This has further threatened jobs in industries in advanced countries which in turn has brought great pressures for increased protection. At the same time, a large majority of the world's people cannot afford more than the basic necessities of life, and frequently fail to reach even this level. Trade in commodities, however, is less concerned with providing the means for everyone to lead healthy lives, than with the ability to pay.

The polarisation of global income and wealth is a substantial challenge to advanced countries. Their sense of responsibility to provide development aid has been eroded by deficits and unemployment at home. However, this aid is the only hope that many impoverished societies have. There is little doubt, either, that greasing the wheels of global commerce and production by fostering economic development in the Third World is an important long-term step in increasing market opportunities generally.

There have been some developments that offer new and very big markets. Some of the less developed economies of the world (mainly in Asia and Latin America) have, by a mixture of reasonably sustained economic development and a shift in prevailing political dogma, managed to progress significantly. The slow emergence of a middle class in such countries means a perceptible development of market demand. As industries expand, they tend to rely on western machinery, equipment, and skills.

In the North American context, Canada's future remains closely tied to that of its American neighbour. Enhanced trade between two of the world's most prosperous economies, whether we like it or not, is one of the few alternatives open during a time of greater protectionism and the increase of other mutual trading blocs. It is an alternative which will occupy the minds of many Canadians for years to come.

Public Debt

Governments at all levels in Canada face a bleak future of accumulated debt, and the equally daunting prospect of reducing this debt. Up to the 1970s, deficits were an acceptable means of managing economic activity, especially during recession. During this time, the network of social support programs was developed, and demands on the public purse increased accordingly. While interest rates were low, accumulation of debt was less of a concern. High interest rates since the late 1970s have meant that some 30% of federal revenues in Canada go to service loans to cover deficits. The provinces have been caught in a similar trap.

Reduction of debt is difficult. Governments must either reduce spending, or increase income. The former can be achieved only by offering fewer services, by offering the same level of services to fewer people, or by more efficient delivery of services. The latter can be achieved by raising taxes, or by levying charges for services usually regarded as being available free. In reality, a combination of all these has been tried, but much remains to be done.

None of these measures is politically attractive, and the resolve to reduce debt suffers accordingly. Increasing taxes or imposing charges for services also reduces disposable incomes, and removes the ability to save or consume commercial products and services. Tax rates in the Atlantic region are already the highest in Canada and are combined with lower-than-average incomes, higher- than-average unemployment, and an economy more vulnerable to swings in the business cycle. Governments are already examining current and future demand for certain services (especially health) in light of an aging population. These intractable problems are unlikely to go away before the end of the century, and they form a sobering part of the Atlantic future.

Environmental Concerns

The emergence of the modern environmental movement during the 1960s and 1970s was a natural outgrowth of economic prosperity; the movement developed because we could afford it, and a new, highly-educated, influential and articulate generation insisted on due regard for our natural surroundings and the plant and animal species that share them with us. Many industries opposed any movement towards environmental controls, which were seen as likely to increase costs of production and pose threats to profits.

Governments, however, recognised their responsibilities early and set up departments and agencies to monitor environmental quality, enact legislation to punish offenders, and try to restore some of the worst excesses that had occurred. Since these new initiatives came after many years of abuse, they could do no more than start correcting degradation while raising public awareness of the problems involved.

The environmental movement of the 1980s is mature and sophisticated. In some parts of Europe it has become a political force with parliamentary representation. There is increasing recognition of the fact that society's economic progress and environmental stewardship are not contradictory but strongly interdependent and complementary. Part of the reason for this is the eventual costs of restoration, societal health, and overall demand for clean air, water, and surroundings.

This holds true particularly in Atlantic Canada, where much industry is solidly based on renewable resources, including the important tourist sector. Many thousands of jobs, and billions of dollars in output and income depend closely on environmental integrity in the region. In some cases (overcut, uneven-aged, decadent or infested forests; inshore shellfish contamination; improper disposal of municipal and industrial wastes; soil erosion in important agricultural areas) there is already considerable damage to repair. Advances in chemical manufacture introduce new and often highly toxic substances to our lives and surroundings every year. Acid precipitation slowly kills lakes, forests, and farmland.

The slowness with which environmental improvements occur make them unattractive to shorter-term political and corporate plans. In fact, entire industries have emerged, and are still forming, around the business of repairing or cleaning up environmental damage. A large majority of North Americans consistently makes environmental issues a high priority for government spending in public opinion polls. This is not likely to change over the coming years; indeed concern is likely to increase and become better organised. Atlantic Canadians, aware of the relative environmental integrity of much of their physical surroundings, will support this movement.

Sector Futures

These broader areas of concern affect industry in Atlantic Canada more or less directly and with varying intensity. Some of this variation relates to the special concerns of individual sectors.

Agriculture. Atlantic farmers will face problems of low prices (at least periodically) and static demand for their products. The entire primary sector in Canada is undergoing adjustment in the late 1980s, and this will take some time to accomplish. The farmers who survive will be quite highly specialised (but not necessarily bigger) or will have combined farming with some form of non-farm income-generating activity. It is difficult to predict too far into the future. Population around the globe increases rapidly, yet most cannot afford the prices required to keep a Canadian farmer in the market.

Emphasis within the primary sector will change from an orientation towards production to an emphasis on marketing. In some cases this will see specialisation depending on small, local markets that demand high quality, fresh and chemical-free food. The spread of farmers' markets will assist this trend. Capital-intense operations, however, will continue to be the rule, possibly with some farms being run by food-processing corporations. Agricultural research will increasingly emphasise the applications of biotechnology.

The Fishery. More sophisticated boats, some but not all bigger, will characterise the Atlantic fishery. Resource constraints will see more emphasis on non-traditional species, especially if new markets in less developed countries emerge. The late 1980s have already seen tastes change to the extent that fish is now regarded as a healthy source of protein, and this trend will continue. Canada's generally good record of stock management will bear dividends in sustaining catches, and more emphasis on a system of property rights in the fishery will assist this process. Quality is already greatly improved, and further improvements are likely as on-boat and dockside handling and storage get better.

Aquaculture has become a feature of the Atlantic fishery for species such as salmon, mussels, and oysters. The region's experience in, and commitment to, aquaculture, however, pales beside that in parts of the world such as the Far East, Norway, and even British Columbia. Biotechnology will make aquaculture more of a commercial and risk-free enterprise, especially in terms of controlling diseases amongst fish.

Forestry. Short- and medium-term difficulties with fibre supply should not blind us to the fact that trees grow well, if slowly, in Atlantic Canada. Reforestation of many cut-over areas will slowly bring the Atlantic woods back. This will incorporate research into species that resist diseases and insect infestation, as well as give the high quality fibre mills demand. Once again, biotechnology will be important.

Pulp and paper competition around the world will be intense, with new production from the Third World based on large reserves of rapidly growing trees. In this respect, although trees may grow slowly in Canada, they offer a high-quality fibre sometimes lacking in warmer-climate species. As well, newly modernised mills in Atlantic Canada are well placed to compete in the world's most important markets. Forestry concerns have an important influence on overall environmental health, and recycling paper may form a bigger part of the industry in the future.

Mining. The future of Atlantic Canada's mines and quarries depends on quality and quantity of reserves, their accessibility, global competition, and emergence of substitute materials. The last of these will be a major influence, as new technologies improve the acceptability of such things as plastics in the manufacture of a wide range of products, and discover further substitutes. Recycling of metals is likely to become more common as environmental issues gain momentum.

Energy. The volatile world of energy prices has been a case study of economics in action since the early 1970s, and remains influenced to a large degree by geopolitical developments. In spite of big variations in price, there is likely to be a steady increase in price overall which will eventually see oil and gas off Newfoundland and Nova Scotia brought ashore.

Electricity generation will also continue to play an important part in regional development, especially in Labrador. Sales of power to American utilities will be a big component of decisions to invest in new capacity. The advent of superconductors has special relevance to energy production and transmission, as this new technology means that no energy is lost during transmission. Eventually, superconductor rings will allow storage of energy close to point of consumption, allowing utilities to even out base and peak load capacities.

Manufacturing. A big part of Atlantic Canada's future will depend on the diversification from a relatively narrow, resource-based manufacturing sector into a wider range of higher-value end products. This will be assisted by better transportation and communications. New technologies have rapidly been adopted by many of the world's most successful manufacturing economies, and will increasingly come to Atlantic industry. Computers (both to help run production lines, and to make research and development work easier) will be an integral part of this process. The further automation of production lines will confer benefits on traditional industries such as fish processing.

Services. Increase of the service sector has characterised North American economies since 1945, and Atlantic Canada is no exception to this rule. A substantial public presence has a pervasive influence on the sector, and gives it an enhanced role in the region. Future expansion of services will depend, in part, on more exports. This is easier for some types of service (such as professional consulting or certain financial services) than for others (such as retail trade). The rise of new types of service industries, including computer services and information management, will make more exports possible. The diversity and dynamism of the entire service sector assures it an important role in Atlantic Canada, and a valuable source of incomes and jobs.

Tourism. A more discerning type of tourist, usually more affluent, will demand a wider range of attractions, and will be willing to pay more for them. A glance at the travel pages of newspapers in the late 1980s reveals how much the nature of the industry has already expanded. Traditional and familiar destinations or experiences now jostle for the tourist dollar with new, frequently remote and exotic destinations. Better transportation networks have made access to such places easier, especially for North Americans.

Atlantic tourism will remain rooted in its traditional attractions of sandy beaches and scenery, with the four provinces perhaps beginning to appreciate the benefits of joint promotions and marketing. Specialist tourism, which is just emerging in the region, will increasingly exploit the different and sometimes unique opportunities to be found in Atlantic Canada. Natural history and "adventure" tours (whale watching, tours to bird islands, viewing seals, and so on) will be a part of this trend. Once again, the importance of environmental health is emphasised.

Transportation and Communications. Rapidly evolving technologies have typified telecommunications in the late twentieth century, and this is not likely to abate. Personal access to much of these advances will make new enterprises possible. More "traditional" industries, as well, will benefit from the greatly enhanced access to most world markets with more use of containers for shipping products, round-the-world services, and easy access to these services through good deepwater ports in the region. Better information, which comes from better communications, is an important part of overall business success.

Atlantic Canada Today . . . and Tomorrow

Despite its economic disparities relative to other parts of Canada and North America, Atlantic Canada is regarded through the eyes of most people in the world as a privileged place to live. Its rich resource base continues to support a relatively diverse economy, and most people have a standard of living beyond the reach and aspirations of most people. This is supplemented by a lifestyle that is itself a product of the natural attractions of the region and its heritage.

Many of the economic challenges that face the region (reducing unemployment and government debt; increasing investment and incomes) are, by their nature, longer-term goals. Society and its elected representatives, impatient for results, only rarely recognise this. Economic and social adjustment, it must be recognised, takes time. As the region approaches the twenty-first century, it can look forward to many positive prospects, as long as the realisation of these prospects is undertaken resolutely and with confidence.

The richness of Atlantic Canada's past gives a good indication of the resourcefulness of its people, frequently in distressing circumstances. This has bred a depth of character which enables them to persevere, and a sense of community which is the envy of others. This is an integral part of the region's future.

Further Reading

Barney, G.O., P.H. Freeman and C.A. Ulinski, *Global 2000: Implications for Canada*. Pergamon Press, Toronto, 1983.

Betcherman, G. and K. McMullen, *Working with Technology: A Survey of Automation in Canada*. Economic Council of Canada. Ottawa, 1986.

Courchene, T.J., *Social Policy in the 1990s: Agenda for Reform.* C.D. Howe Institute, Policy Study No. 3. Montreal, Calgary and Toronto, 1987.

Eaton, P.B., L.P. Hildebrand and A.A. d'Entremont, *Environmental Quality in the Atlantic Region 1985.* Environment Canada, Atlantic Region. Dartmouth, 1986.

The Economist, "Factory of the Future". May 30, 1987.

Index

Index   **201**

insurance, 131
Intercolonial railway, 8
International Commission for the Northwest Atlantic Fisheries, 47
interprovincial trade barriers, 187n
investments, 105–7, 110–11, 190, 197
Irish, 16
iron ore, 76, 77, 83, 97, 147, 180

Keynesian economics, 123

labour force, 119, 158–9; composition, 164; educational levels, 165; participation rates, 158, 159–164, 170, 173; women in, 159, 164–5
labour supply, 157
Labrador, 1, 3, 65
Labrador City, 75
Labrador Current, 3
"land-bridging", 149
land classification, 42n
language, 17
Laurier, Sir Wilfrid, 184
lead, 75, 77, 80, 180
Liverpool, N.S., 149
lobster, 47, 48, 52, 54, 59
logs, 67, 68, 177, 180
Louisbourg, N.S., 6
Loyalists, 7
lumber, 67, 68
lumber industry, 65
Lunenburg County, N.S., 17, 29

mackerel, 59
Mactaquac hydro station, 87
manpower policies, 157, 173
manufacturing, 23, 97–103, 129, 151, 185; concentration in Ontario, 101; forest-based, 68; ownership, 101, 102; value added, 97; value of goods, 99
manufacturing plants, 99
maple, 65
Marconi, Gugliemo, 153–4
marketing boards, 38–40
Maritime Command, 133
Maritime Freight Rates Act (MFRA), 120, 148, 150, 151
Maritime Rights Movement, 8, 120, 150
Maritime provinces: defined, 1
Marx, Karl, 127
medical services, 190
mercantilism, 7, 176
microwave networks, 153, 154
midshore fishery, 52
midshore fishing fleet, 54
military, 23, 133
mineral exploration, 82
mineral production, 77, 81–2
minerals: competition between producers, 80, 81; criteria for extraction, 75, 79–80; export, 77; markets, 81; prices, 80–1; strategic importance, 81; value, 82–3
mine closure, 80, 89
mine ownership, 77, 79
mining, 75–83, 189, 195; labour costs, 8; technology, 81
Ministry of State of Economic and Regional Development, 122
molybdenum, 77, 79
Moncton, N.B., 16
Mount Carleton, 4

National Sea Products, 58
neoclassical economic theory, 123
New Brunswick: agriculture, 27, 28, 29, 38; doctors and dentists, 19; employment, 166; energy supply, 87; ethnic background of population, 16; exports, 180, 182; farm cash receipts, 35; farms, 30; fishery, 52; forestry, 65, 67; labour supply, 152; language, 17; manufacturing, 99–100; mining, 75, 77, 79; population, 13; physical features, 2, 4; productivity, 107; telephones, 154; tourism, 136, 137; soils, 29; unemployment, 170; wages and incomes, 116, 173
New England, 17, 87, 90
Newfoundland and Labrador: agriculture, 28, 29, 38; doctors and dentists, 19; employment, 166; energy supply, 87, 89; exports, 180; farm cash receipts, 34–5; farms, 30; fishery, 48; fisherman, 53; fishing boats, 54; forestry, 65, 67; labour supply, 158; mnaufacturing, 99–100; mining, 75, 76, 77, 81; population, 13; productivity, 107; service industries, 127; settlement, 6; telephones, 155; tourism, 136, 137; soils, 29; unemployment, 169, 170; unions, 171, 173; wages and incomes, 116, 173
newspapers, 152
newsprint, 65, 68, 100, 180, 184

Index   **203**

Index   **205**